Praise for *Stuck*

"This book is simply outstanding, and it comes to us not a minute too soon. Pastors will find this research not only invaluable but also a healing balm for their souls. With laser-like precision, Ferguson and Packard name the primary factors afflicting pastors today, and I have never felt so understood. I am deeply grateful for the insights contained in these pages, which were personally illuminating and filled me with hope."

—Sharon Hodde Miller, teaching pastor,
Bright City Church, Durham, NC

"*Stuck* offers a poignant and important sociological analysis of a growing crisis in Christian life: the alienation of clergy from their callings. Given the importance of clergy in helping all Christians discover their callings in diverse vocations, this crisis cries out for the kind of urgent attention and action reflected in Ferguson and Packard's analysis."

—L. Gregory Jones, president, Belmont University; coauthor of *Resurrecting Excellence: Shaping Faithful Christian Ministry*

"This book should be required reading at any seminary that aims to prepare ministers for the challenges ahead. Beautifully written with unmistakable compassion for pastors and their congregations, Ferguson and Packer's book shows us that pastors feel stuck not because of spiritual failings but because of changing economic, social, organizational, and cultural realities that make their job seem impossible. Though the calling to ministry needn't change, the pastoring profession must change. Ferguson and Packard tell us why, then show us how."

—Samuel L. Perry, associate professor of sociology
and religious studies, University of Oklahoma

"Ever felt like larger forces were at play and you just couldn't name them clearly? *Stuck* unveils the underestimated forces affecting clergy and offers an unforgettable framework that just might help clergy get unstuck."

—Rae Jean Proeschold-Bell, research director, Duke Clergy Health Initiative; research professor, Duke Global Health Institute

"This week, as I finished reading Ferguson and Packard's *Stuck*, *Christianity Today* magazine posted a headline: 'The Pastors Aren't All Right: 38% Consider Leaving Ministry.' Not only does this book beautifully explain why pastors aren't all right, but it also explains why so many consider leaving ministry but ultimately only *consider* leaving. In a helpful mixture of sociology and practical theology, these authors offer a description of the problems their research respondents face but, with the questions they pose to pastors and congregations, also push both parties to consider solutions. An important book about spiritual burnout, this should be week-one assigned reading in any training environment for clerical aspirants."

—Richard Pitt, author of *Divine Callings: Understanding the Call to Ministry in Black Pentecostalism* and *Church Planters: Inside the World of Religion Entrepreneur*

"In this valuable volume, sociologists Ferguson and Packard examine and explain why a growing number of Protestant clergy feel stuck in ministry—wanting and even needing to leave the places and people they lead. As one who leads a seminary that educates and equips God-called people for gospel ministry in and alongside the church, I found *Stuck* simultaneously sobering and illuminating. This book will inform and transform the way I seek to serve and to shape ministers."

—Todd D. Still, Baylor University, Truett Seminary

STUCK

STUCK

Why **Clergy** Are Alienated from Their
Calling, Congregation, and Career
... and What to Do about It

Todd W. Ferguson

Josh Packard

FORTRESS PRESS
MINNEAPOLIS

Cover design: Kris Miller

Print ISBN: 978-1-5064-8083-1
eBook ISBN: 978-1-5064-8084-8

To the clergy, those thriving and those stuck

Contents

Illustrations

Preface

This book began with a conversation. I (Packard) was leading the Dechurched Project analyzing the dones—those who had left the church but not their faith.[1] The project was meant to focus on only the laity, but pastors kept reaching out to me because they too were "done." I wasn't sure what to do with these pastors. They seemed desperate for help and eager to find a way to tell their stories, but they did not fit the scope of this research. I mentioned this to Todd while we were both at the annual meeting of the Society for the Scientific Study of Religion, the yearly gathering of sociologists, psychologists, and other social scientists who study religion. The two of us were empathetic to the situation that these clergy found themselves in and yet perplexed. Why would a pastor be done with the very institution he or she leads? Is this burnout or something else? How can we help them? We knew we had to do something to help these pastors reaching out to us. The Stuck Pastor Project was born.

All research is biography in many ways. As scholars, we often study the topics that are closest to us personally. This book was written because pastors are dear to us. The two of us study religion from a sociological viewpoint, and we are particularly interested in congregations. I (Packard) studied the emerging church for my dissertation before diving into why laypeople leave the church in my book *Church Refugees*.[2] I currently lead the Springtide Research Institute, which examines the spiritual and social lives of young people. I (Ferguson) was a local pastor before I became a sociologist. After graduating with my MDiv (master of divinity) from Duke Divinity School, I was the associate pastor at Willow Meadows Baptist Church in Houston, Texas, a thoughtful, loving congregation affiliated with the Cooperative Baptist Fellowship and the Baptist General Convention of Texas. While I would not consider myself a "stuck pastor," my experience in the ministry deepened my empathy for those leading congregations.

Congregations matter and so do their pastors. When pastors are waving a flag signaling that something is wrong, we need to listen. We need to listen as social scientists, but also, and more importantly, we need to listen as congregants, church council members, and denominational and seminary leaders. We need to listen as both the people served by these clergy and the people charged with serving and supporting them.

We decided to begin a project to study "stuck pastors" for those who did not want to be congregational pastors any longer but did not know where to turn. They felt stuck leading the very organizations that they wanted to leave. Our goal for this project is to offer a voice to these pastors so they know they are not alone and they are not "crazy." Yet we also want to do more than just tell their stories. We want to provide a theoretical, sociological explanation for why pastors are going through this experience. By doing so, we hope to show that this situation is larger than any one pastor. Powerful social forces are affecting congregations, denominations, and religion writ large. Clergy are at the forefront of these changes. The personal feeling of being stuck for them is truly a microcosm of what is going on in North American religion.

HOW WE CONDUCTED OUR STUDY

Our study was not unlike many other qualitative examinations. We were drawn to interviews and qualitative data for this topic because that methodology is better suited to it than the quantitative data obtained through surveys. While quantitative data are excellent for telling us "what" is happening, it is the qualitative data that can shed light on "how" or "why" something is happening. For a topic interwoven with secrecy, shame, identity, and other complex issues, it is important to establish the "how" and "why."

However, we should not give the impression that we entered into interviews and data collection without strategies, hypotheses, or goals. We assumed we would find familiar stories about burnout or even loss of faith, both of which are common in the scientific literature about pastors. However, the findings from this book largely result from our formulating hypotheses based on that scientific literature about pastors (e.g., pastors burn out over time)—and then finding out that our hypotheses were wrong.

Respondents were recruited via Twitter and Facebook utilizing both personal networks and paid advertisements. We had initially hoped to rely heavily on chain referral, or what is sometimes called "snowball" sampling. This way of identifying potential interviewees is typically useful when it comes to accessing populations who might be difficult to reach. People tend to know others like them. However, we found this strategy to be less successful than we had hoped, pointing to just how isolated pastors are who are struggling with their calling or are thinking about making a change. They often knew of nobody else who was experiencing the same thing, at least not openly. This initial roadblock pushed us toward recruiting via social media, which proved far more successful.

In the appendix, you can see our interview guide, and readers with a social science background will likely be able to map particular questions back to specific research articles and theories about clergy wellness, burnout, and loss of faith. It's important to note that this instrument evolved significantly over time, however. While the vast majority of questions were consistent even as we modified our interviews, we used the guide as more of a reminder about the information we wanted to collect than as a structured protocol we rigidly followed from question 1 to question 2 and so on. Prior to any interview, respondents signed an informed consent document and were promised anonymity. There was no compensation or other exchange for their participation. In the end, they simply wanted to tell their stories. And they wanted someone to listen.

Good qualitative research relies a great deal on establishing rapport with the person you are interviewing while retaining enough critical distance to be able to ask challenging and clarifying questions. Thus it was not uncommon for a respondent to launch into a twenty-minute or longer history of how they came to be a pastor that answered a lot of the questions in our interview guide, even if the story was not told in the order that we had written out those questions. Along the way, we were making notes so we could double back, challenge assumptions, test theories, and seek commonalities with other interviews that had already been collected and analyzed.

After we transcribed the interviews, we coded them multiple times looking for common themes using computer software to help us keep track of everything and make the analysis systematic as opposed to haphazard. We had assistance in this effort from graduate students for training and triangulation purposes, but we both were invested heavily in this process. We coded both for the theories and hypotheses that shaped our interview guide based on our background reading and for emergent themes and patterns that were common to our respondents but had largely gone unnoticed by scholars up to this point.

All researchers bring elements of subjectivity to their projects. Whether dealing with numbers and quantitative evidence or words and qualitative data, our own biases inevitably creep in. Rather than try to pretend we could don "white coats" and clinically distance ourselves from the data collection, analysis, and write-up, we explicitly own that we care deeply about our respondents and their profession. We are sympathetic to their struggle. And we are also social scientists who care a great deal about finding what is objectively true. With this positionality in mind, then, we always endeavored to not only understand our data sociologically but also uncover what the implications of those findings would be for the profession and the church at large.[3]

OUR INTERVIEWEES

In total, we conducted forty-two interviews with Protestant clergy from Canada and the United States. Our sample is by no means representative of all clergy. Qualitative research, like the in-depth interviews we conducted, will never be representative, but then again, that is not its goal. As shown in table P.1, our interviewees were mostly men, but more than one-quarter were women. This percentage within our study is larger than the 10 percent of all head clergy in the United States who are women, but our sample includes associate pastors and other ministers who are not senior leaders.[4] Twenty-one of the pastors (50 percent) we spoke to are still serving as full-time pastors, and two are serving part time. Two others had returned to college to continue their nontheological education by the time we interviewed them. One pastor had retired, and one other was in noncongregational ministry. Almost 25 percent of our interviewees (ten) were in secular employment outside the ministry, while four former pastors were unemployed and could not find work. We struggled to categorize one interviewee's employment, and so we labeled this person's professional position as "unknown."

As with most clergy, our sample is highly educated. Over half have a graduate degree, most often the MDiv. Only four of our interviewees did not have a college education. Thirty-three of our pastors (78.6 percent) were married, and one was partnered in a same-sex relationship. Five were either divorced or separated, one was single, and two did not discuss their relationship status.

Table P.1: Demographic characteristics

	N	Percent
Total interviewees	*42*	
Gender		
Men	31	73.8
Women	11	26.2
Position		
Full-time pastor	21	50.0
Part-time pastor	2	4.8
Other ministry	1	2.4
Furthering education	2	4.8
Retired	1	2.4
Secular employment	10	23.8
Unemployed	4	9.5
Unknown	1	2.4

	N	Percent
Education		
High school diploma	1	2.4
Some college	3	7.1
Bachelor's degree	12	28.6
Master of divinity	23	54.8
Other master's	1	2.4
Doctor of ministry	2	4.8
Marital status		
Married	33	78.6
Partnered	1	2.4
Divorced	4	9.5
Separated	1	2.4
Single	1	2.4
Unknown	2	4.8
Religious tradition		
Evangelical Protestant	23	54.8
Mainline Protestant	18	42.9
Other religious tradition	1	2.4
Age range	33–67	
Household income range (in USD)	$22,000–$145,000	

In terms of religious traditions, twenty-three (54.8 percent) of our pastors were Evangelical Protestants, and eighteen (42.9 percent) were Mainline Protestants. One interviewee categorized himself as being from another religious tradition, though he formerly was an Evangelical pastor. As the following list shows, a range of denominations is represented among these Mainline and Evangelical pastors:

- American Baptist Churches
- Church of God (Cleveland, TN)
- Church of the Nazarene
- Churches of Christ
- Episcopal Church
- Evangelical Covenant Church
- Evangelical Lutheran Church of America
- Evangelical Missionary Church of Canada
- Independent Baptist
- Mennonite Church Canada
- Nondenominational
- Presbyterian Church (U.S.A.)
- Presbyterian Church in Canada
- Southern Baptist Convention
- The Foursquare Church
- United Church of Christ
- United Methodist Church
- Vineyard Church

WHERE ARE THE CATHOLIC PRIESTS?

Our sample does not include Catholic priests, but they were not omitted from the study on purpose. As we recruited clergy for our study, we received numerous interview requests to participate from Protestants. We had so many that we eventually stopped interviewing because we felt like we reached a point of data saturation, and we were constrained by time and resources. Yet no Catholic priests responded. Midway through our data collection, we realized the lack of Catholics, and we changed our recruiting tactics. We used grant money from the University of Northern Colorado to fund targeted Facebook ads geared to Catholic priests. We used an image of the clergy collar, typical of priests, in our branding and marketing. None of these efforts worked. We received zero interview requests from Catholics. Why did Catholic priests not respond? Do they not struggle within ministry? We do not think this is the case.

Instead, we believe the lack of priests is the result of a few factors. First, we are outsiders to Roman Catholicism. We are both Protestants. Most of our social networks are within the worlds of both Evangelical and Mainline Protestantism. It is possible that priests were reluctant to speak to us because of this outsider status. A priest who speaks about the struggles of ordained ministry to non-Catholics could possibly interpret this as talking badly about "the family" to someone who is not within "the family."

Second, ordination within Roman Catholicism "costs more" for priests than it does for Protestant ministers. Catholic priests take vows of obedience and chastity, with those who belong to religious orders adding the vow of poverty. These are substantial commitments for a priest. They can be interpreted as "sunk costs," which means priests are less likely to leave the ministry given the level of sacrifices they have made to be ordained.

Third, and we believe most important, the ordained Catholic priesthood is qualitatively different from ordained Protestant ministry. While those within the Anglican tradition are the most similar to Catholics among Protestants, ordination in Roman Catholicism is interpreted as having ontological consequences for the priest. In other words, ordination into the priesthood changes the person's very nature. In his essay on the priesthood, John Cardinal O'Connor writes, "We don't just put on vestments; we don't just receive an assignment. Neither makes us priests. We *become* priests at ordination.

There is an 'ontological change' in our spiritual nature. Such is a profound mystery."[5]

This understanding of the priesthood is radically different from how most Protestant traditions interpret ordination. For some in the free church traditions (Baptists, Pentecostals, nondenominational churches, and the like), ordination—if they practice it at all—merely sets a person apart for spiritual leadership. The liturgical Protestant traditions, like the Episcopal Church and the United Methodist Church, have a more spiritual understanding of the practice, but it comes nowhere close to mysteriously transforming the clergyperson's actual essence. Therefore, we believe that Catholic priests are less likely to respond to a request to interview "pastors who do not want to be pastors anymore." To do so means to doubt one's own essence. For Catholic priests, the ministry is not just a job, but it is who a person is. Many Protestant ministers have this personal view as well, but it is not woven into the theology and liturgy of their traditions. We still believe that there are Catholic priests who want to leave the priesthood because they experience an alienation from their faith or the pressures of organizational survival. Yet their reasons for staying are most likely quite different from Protestants'.

IS THIS BOOK ABOUT LOSING FAITH OR BURNING OUT?

The fact that the role of the pastor and the structure and culture of the congregation can hinder one's call to serve God means that there are pastors who preach the Word and preside at the Table every week but do not want to be there.[6] They want to leave the profession but think they cannot. This book is not about clergy who are dissatisfied with their current positions and want to move to other congregations. That is an entirely different subject, and other scholars have already tackled it well.[7] This is also not a book about clergy losing their faith. While one of our interviewees said that he had lost his faith, most of the pastors in this book continue to be passionate about their spiritual lives. They want to go deeper in their faith but feel like serving in a congregation gets in the way of connecting with God.

In reality, some pastors do lose their faith. There have been some well-known cases, like Joshua Harris, the author of the popular 1990s book *I Kissed Dating Goodbye*, who announced in 2019 that he no longer considered himself Christian.[8] Researchers Daniel Dennett and Linda LaScola have written more about this pattern in their book *Caught in the Pulpit*.[9] These stories are important, and so we do not want to gloss over them. We did not find this pattern often, however. What we did find was that people are called to lead spiritually, but the way ministry is currently structured got in the way of this calling.

This is also not a book about clergy burnout. Burnout is such an important topic within the clergy, and it is a major force that affects pastors.[10] (There is excellent research on clergy burnout, and those interested should follow the work of the Duke Clergy Health Initiative at Duke Divinity School.) Viewing it as a psychological concept, many therapists and psychologists could rightly interpret some of the pastors we spoke to as struggling with this issue. Yet we are sociologists, and our goal is to focus on how the social role of being a pastor and the organizational structure of the congregation can create an environment where it is difficult to follow one's call to serve God. Most of the pastors we spoke to were not burned out. They still had the enthusiasm and commitment to lead spiritually connected lives with others. Their struggle, instead, was to find ways in which to follow God's call in the midst of a role and an organization that often thwarted their efforts.

TWF
Belton, TX

JRP
Greeley, CO

August 2021

INTRODUCTION
Knowing How the Sausage Is Made

I have sometimes thought that, in order to be
a good minister, it was necessary to leave the
ministry.

—Ralph Waldo Emerson, *The Journals and
Miscellaneous Notebooks of Ralph Waldo Emerson*

Marcus is dissatisfied as a pastor.[1] On the surface, he is quite
successful. At thirty-three years old, he is an associate pastor
at a healthy Presbyterian Church (U.S.A.) (PCUSA) in the
South and is happily married with children. Yet every week
the worship services he leads for his church are no longer
spiritual experiences for him. Instead, leading worship is just
one part of his job. He says, "For a long time, it's felt, and it
continues to feel, like it's work. It's . . . what I'm doing for
my job."

This "job" is to create meaningful, spiritual moments
where people can connect with God. He does this faithfully
every week: he reads Scripture, leads Bible studies, writes his
sermons, and plans the music. Yet he does not have spiritual

experiences within the worship services he leads. Instead, he thinks of himself as putting on a show for his congregants. He says, "I've begun to see myself as an actor but not as a participant." He leads his church in worship for the sake of his congregants, but internally, he feels disconnected.

We probed further and asked him if it was the act of *leading* a worship service that created this sense of disconnection. He told us no, that was not the issue. When he participates in another church's worship, he moves from being an actor in the service to becoming a critic: "It's almost worse when I go to another service [as a participant] because then I start looking at how they could be doing things differently and better communicate their message." It is almost like he knows too much of what goes on behind the scenes to create a worship service, and so he uses the cliché "You never want to know how the sausage is made" when he describes his personal participation in worship. His life is not devoid of spirituality, however. He continues to develop his relationship with God privately through studying Scripture and personal prayer. Yet his career is not just to have a private devotional life but to be a public leader in worship. Among the many tasks that pastors do in a week, preparing for and leading worship are central to managing a congregation. On average, those two duties take up at least one-third of their time.[2]

So why does Marcus stay in the ministry? If he cannot connect with God during the very service he leads, why doesn't he go into another career? He offers two reasons: stability and Jesus. The stability of a pastoral position within the PCUSA is quite attractive. As a Mainline Protestant denomination, PCUSA congregations offer a decent salary, good health care, a reliable pension, and benefits such as paid time off and study leave.[3] Even though congregations like his are shrinking, especially within the Mainline tradition, Marcus knows that even dwindling congregations will retain and pay pastors for years. He has put in a lot of time and money to reach this position by graduating from seminary, studying for ordination exams, and seeking a pastoral position. It would be quite difficult to find another career with such benefits. He stays because it is secure.

The second reason he offers—and he states it is secondary—for remaining in the ministry is Jesus. Marcus continues to feel called to lead others toward Christ. He says, "I still do believe very much in the person of Jesus and who Jesus was and how Jesus asks that we live our lives. And I want to try to communicate that as best I can." At the heart of his pastoral career is Christ. Jesus motivates him to work toward bringing about social justice and making the world a better place.

Yet despite the stability of his position and his desire to lead others to Jesus, Marcus questions if a congregation is the setting in which he can follow his calling long term. He differentiates between the "concept of the church as an existing framework" and the church "as this thing that Jesus talked about—this sense of community, of being with people whom you share your beliefs and your views on God with." He absolutely wants to be a part of the church as a community but is unsure about the effectiveness of the church as a "framework" within which people's spiritual lives flourish.

Part of his reluctance to fully support the current model of the congregation is that the people he is serving—his congregants—are the ones who sign his paycheck. They can fire him if they do not like what he is doing. So even though pastors have a lot of freedom in their job, this dynamic causes Marcus to limit his vision for his congregation. He says,

> One of the biggest benefits that you have as a clergy member is that it is almost like being a business owner

or an entrepreneur. You have the ability to run your own shop. But at the same time, there is this catch that the congregation is paying you, and so you withhold some of your visions or your dreams or what you think would be a really good idea because people who are signing your paycheck aren't necessarily completely bought into that—whereas you can try to implement more of those things if you had a little bit more say-so in terms of where your own paycheck was coming from.

To get around this dynamic of trying to both lead his congregants and please them because they hold the power of the purse, Marcus envisions himself earning his living by writing and speaking: "I think ideally, I would like to bypass that entire system if I was able to provide my own set of income either through speaking or preaching or writing. . . . Then it would provide the opportunity to actually get back to the community, be involved in social justice programs, get people to give more to the community at large and toward the mission of the church."

He interprets the congregational model as a constraint on his ministry. If he could rearrange his financial situation so he could earn a salary outside of the traditional congregation, he sees himself as actually freeing himself up to do the work of ministry.

Marcus is extremely ambivalent about his career. He feels a passion for working for social justice issues in the name of Christ, but at the same time, he is completely disconnected from the worship life of his congregation. He wants a stable profession within a congregation but wonders if institutional forms that ensure this stability actually thwart his calling to ministry.

AN OVERTURE

Marcus's experience is an overture for the major theme we will explore in this book: *the role of the pastor and the structure of the congregation can hinder one's call to serve God.* As a result, some pastors feel stuck and are desperate to leave the profession. A few find a way out. They follow their calling outside traditional ministry. Others cannot, and they feel stuck as pastors. In this book, we explore this feeling of being "stuck" in three arenas: (1) stuck in the calling of ministry, (2) stuck in the congregation, and (3) stuck in the career.

Part I of this book examines a challenge pastors face: they are called to be spiritual leaders, but the pastoral role itself can constrain a pastor's own spiritual development. Marcus experiences this problem when he describes how he feels spiritually disconnected from worship because he is the leader of the service. As he says, "I know how the sausage is made." In chapter 1, we call this feeling of disconnection "alienation," which can cause pastors to feel inauthentic as they lead their congregations. Marcus struggles with authenticity because his congregation pays his salary. He withholds aspects of himself, including parts of his faith, because to be open and vulnerable can be too risky for his career. If his congregants do not like what he reveals, they can fire him. Chapter 2 focuses on how pastors have had to redefine their sense of divine calling on their lives in order to remain authentic. Most of the clergy we spoke to continue to feel a powerful sense of calling on their lives to serve God, but they wonder if congregational ministry can sustain this calling.

Part II investigates how pastors' issues are more than personal or spiritual—they are organizational as well. Pastors not only need to lead worship or Bible studies, but they must focus on the business-related aspects of their congregations, such as budgets and membership numbers. If they ignore the business part of their churches, these congregations can close. This pressure to ensure organizational survival can actually get in the way of spiritual growth, so some pastors view the congregational structure as an impediment to living out their calling, a pattern we will investigate in chapter 3. Marcus is also serving in the PCUSA. Among the interviewees, Mainline pastors especially felt the pressure of congregational survival because of their denominations' historic decline in numbers since the 1960s. Therefore, we will focus particularly on Mainline clergy in chapter 4 to examine their experiences of leading organizations in the midst of shrinking resources and declining churches.

Part III asks the question, "Why don't these pastors just leave if they are so unhappy?" The fact that Marcus has not left the ministry for another career is important. He cites staying because of both a calling and financial stability. In chapter 5, we will explore the forces that keep dissatisfied clergy in the ministry, paying particular attention to the social stigma that comes with being a member of the clergy and the financial stability that a professional job brings. Finally, in chapter 6, we will follow the stories of the pastors who have "left the ministry" and begun other careers. These former pastors often interpret their exits from the pastoral role explicitly as a way of more faithfully following their call to serve God.

For each chapter, we offer questions for reflection and discussion to both pastors and the leaders and staff of major institutions that sustain the pastorate: churches, seminaries, and denominations. Our hope is that each chapter is the starting point for a larger conversation about how to create and sustain a healthy ministry.

This book's major premise—*the role of the pastor and the structure of the congregation can hinder one's call to serve*

God—does not mean that every pastor is miserable or that the typical organizational form of a congregation is terrible and impedes spiritual growth. We do not argue this, because we do not believe this. Many pastors absolutely love their roles and are thriving. Congregations too can be life-giving organizations that have the potential to nurture people's faith and work for justice in their communities. We do not overgeneralize a doom-and-gloom scenario for the entire area of ministry. Instead, our objective is more nuanced. We are trying to demonstrate that, given the current context of North American religion situated within capitalism and secularization, there is a potential dark side to our current understanding of the pastoral role and the function of the congregation. We want to recognize that there are clergy who are crying out for help in their ministries, often unable to share their pain with others. We hope this book allows these pastors to understand that they are not alone.

THE SOCIAL CONTEXT OF MINISTRY IN THE TWENTY-FIRST CENTURY

The job of a pastor in a congregation is not an isolated social phenomenon. It does not exist on its own, independent of other social forces. This role is embedded within the larger cultural and structural context of religion in North America. In the twenty-first century, three major forces are shaping religion: (1) social Darwinism, (2) capitalism, and (3) secularization.

SOCIAL DARWINISM

Congregations in the United States and Canada operate within the rules of social Darwinism: the survival of the fittest. Because neither of these two countries has an official state church, religious groups must take on the form of voluntary associations.[4] No governmental agencies or other large entities will support them. Congregations, and their pastors, must recruit enough members and resources or these organizations will die. As voluntary associations, no one is forced to join. The congregation, and by extension the pastor, must be appealing enough to bring in members. This means that pastors face enormous pressures to act and preach in ways that attract members—and their money—to their congregations. Moreover, the pastor's paycheck comes directly from the congregation in most Protestant denominations. This dynamic dramatically alters the nature of the pastoral role. Ministers feel constrained in what they do, what they can say, and how hard they can push to help people grow spiritually. If they step out of line or push too hard, there could be disastrous financial repercussions.

Social Darwinism also means that the success or failure of pastors' congregations is perceived as being up to them. If a church grows and thrives, people view the pastor as a good leader. If it shrinks, or even shuts down, it is the pastor's fault. The clergy we spoke to intuitively understood this dynamic for the pastoral role, and it has enormous consequences.

CAPITALISM

Second and relatedly, capitalism has left its deep mark on the church. Congregations are situated within a system whose sole goal is the creation of profit. The language and practices of congregations reflect this. We hear talk of people "church shopping" or churches being "seeker friendly," reflecting the idea that congregants are consumers of churches' offerings. Churches "market" themselves using advertising campaigns because they are religion's sellers. Scholars studying American religion understood capitalism's impact on churches even back in the 1960s. When describing the immense changes that were occurring in religious life in the middle of the twentieth century, the sociologist Peter Berger wrote then, "Religious institutions become marketing agencies and the religious traditions become consumer commodities."[5] Because our society is shaped by capitalism, we tend to view corporations as the ideal type of organization. It is the business—and not the congregation—that is the model for how respectable and legitimate organizations should be. And so congregations will adopt both the practices found in the business world (e.g., efficiency) and its goals (e.g., growth) in order to be successful. The role of a pastor is transformed by this thinking—from shepherding a congregation in faith to leading as a CEO with a strategic vision for growth and development. Titles such as "executive pastor" and the myriad of church leadership books that recommend adopting a business model to ensure success demonstrate capitalism's pervasive influence on congregations and denominations. Many of the pastors we spoke to understood capitalism's power and viewed these business practices as being antithetical to spiritual growth.

SECULARIZATION

Finally, the role of the pastor and the structure of the congregation are profoundly affected by the process of secularization, or the decline of religion.[6] The religious landscape in North America is forever being changed because more people are leaving organized religion. This means people are both less likely to say they belong to a religious group and less likely to attend worship services.[7] Social scientists often call a person who no longer affiliates with any religion a none. When asked on surveys "What is your religious preference?" these individuals select the option "None," and it is estimated that around 25 percent of Americans and Canadians are nones.[8]

The increase in the nones is a twofold setback for religious congregations because a shrinking number of people who say they are religious results in lower rates of worship attendance and membership. First, there are fewer people who might join, be active, and contribute to congregations, making their long-term survival more difficult. Second, congregations lose social status within society because a smaller proportion of the population even identifies with the groups' faith. As the percentage of people who are religious shrinks, religious organizations are no longer one of the core institutions in society and stand only on the periphery of social life.

Even among North Americans who belong to a religious group (and therefore are not nones), fewer are attending worship services. In 2018, almost a third of the United States (30 percent) never attended worship,[9] while around 54 percent of Canadians reported they either seldom or never attended.[10] Sociologists have teased the data even further and found that the decline in worship attendance does not stem from individuals reducing their level of religious commitment over their lifetime. Instead, the decline comes from generational replacement.[11] Older, more religiously committed people die and are replaced by younger, less religious cohorts.

This decline in personal behavior is happening at the individual level, but congregations are also experiencing a "concentration effect" at the organizational level: more people are attending larger congregations, and smaller churches are shrinking or even dying.[12] The median number of total people participating in congregations has decreased over the past twenty years from 150 to 130.[13] Most congregations are small and getting smaller.

Yet those numbers do not tell the whole story. As sociologist Mark Chaves, the director of the National Congregations Study, aptly puts it, "Most congregations are small, but most people are in large congregations."[14] The average person worships in a congregation of around 650 to 700 people. This pattern increasingly concentrates more worshippers in fewer congregations. This means that a minority of congregations are large and well resourced, while the remainder have plateaued, are shrinking, or are even on the brink of closing. This concentration effect will have dramatic financial implications for the current model of congregations being served by professional, full-time clergy. Clergy in large congregations will have high salaries with good benefits. Many pastors, unfortunately, will not be able to find sustainable positions because most congregations are too small to support a full-time pastor.

Because of these three powerful social forces in North American religion—social Darwinism, capitalism, and secularization—pastors face a precarious situation. They must lead within a context where congregations compete with one another (social Darwinism) for an increasingly smaller supply of potential members (secularization), and yet the standard of their success is numerical growth (capitalism). Some pastors succeed in this marketplace, but as we will show, this success often comes at the cost of feeding the demands of a spirit-deadening bureaucracy. Pastors who cannot "succeed" by growing their congregations risk being fired or shutting down their churches, and so they must ask if the professional ministry can sustain their calling to be spiritual leaders.

PERSONAL TROUBLES AND PUBLIC ISSUES

The sociologist C. Wright Mills notes that many of the problems that individuals face are not personal "troubles" but instead society-wide "issues."[15] The astute observer of society must be able to see the societal impact on the individual. When pastors struggle in the ministry, people often look for psychological burnout, a loss of faith, or some personality defect. But personal troubles are themselves situated within larger social forces. No single pastor can change how capitalism shapes congregational ministry or stop the consequences of secularization, but individual pastors are often held accountable for their outcomes. As a result, while these social forces are beyond the individual control of pastors, they feel very personal. They create an environment where clergy can feel stuck.

Pastors feel stuck within a calling that drives them to be spiritual leaders only to find that congregational ministry alienates them from their own faith. They are stuck within their congregations, the very organizations formed to develop communities' faith in God. Churches become mired in bureaucracy or wrapped up in institutional maintenance, which squeezes the Spirit out of the churches' lives. In the wake of sex abuse scandals and overall secularization, clergy find that the word *pastor* on their résumés carries a powerful negative stigma, and the transition to another career is fraught with difficulties. These pastors feel stuck within their careers and unable to get out.

This book gives voice to these stuck pastors. We hope and pray that the stories we share allow other stuck pastors to better understand what they are feeling and why. They are not alone, and this is not an isolated, individual problem. Being stuck is not the result of personal defects but comes from society-wide issues that create the uncertain world in which pastors now lead their congregations.

PART I
STUCK IN THE CALLING

CHAPTER 1

THE PASTORAL ROLE AND THE ALIENATION OF FAITH

In short, we ordain only the safe parts of our preachers. The dangerous parts—their struggles, wanderings, doubts, and sin—we kindly ask them to leave in the parking lot.
—A. J. Swoboda, *The Dusty Ones*

Marshall was a youth pastor at a wealthy suburban megachurch in the South. By the standards of many, he was very successful. His youth group was gigantic, almost a congregation in its own right. The youth ministry had four youth worship services every weekend, plus a service for college students. There was an entirely separate building for the teenagers and a large staff to help coordinate the ministry. To attract youth, he would invite minor movie stars or give away cruise vacation packages at their big events. And it worked. There was a lot of energy in the ministry, and teenagers flocked to his church.

And yet Marshall was physically, mentally, and spiritually exhausted. He would arrive at the church at seven o'clock on Sunday mornings to prepare for the three morning youth services and would not get home until ten o'clock at night, after the college service ended. He describes his summers—his most busy season, when the teenagers were out of school—saying, "There were summers where I would literally be home for one week. And that's if you count just Saturdays. One Saturday here, one Saturday there, one week. Like seven days maybe for the whole summer between mission trips and summer camps and whatever. That's just not healthy—not for a soul of an individual, not for a marriage definitely."

He questioned whether his gigantic youth ministry actually produced faithful Christians or if it provided only an entertaining distraction for hundreds of teenagers each week. Marshall describes his feelings during that period by saying, "I begin to get bitter at a larger church and what it is producing. . . . I want to focus more in on disciples. When we graduate a student, I want him or her to look a little more like 'I know what the Bible is. I know what it says. I know what I believe before I head off to college.'"

This bitterness was at the core of Marshall's dilemma. He did not know if the ministry he led only created a well-produced, entertaining show or if it shaped teenagers into devoted followers of Christ.

His cynicism with the megachurch reached a breaking point one Easter morning. The congregation hosted twelve worship services to accommodate forty-five thousand people, and the youth ministry was given the task of managing the parking lots. The teenagers would guide the Easter worshippers from their cars to the sanctuary. Marshall remembers that he was standing in the middle of a crosswalk helping direct traffic and pedestrians. He looked up and saw his two daughters in their new Easter dresses in the crowd. One of them ran up to him and hugged his legs, but as he recalls it, this wasn't a happy memory of a family being together on an important religious day: "I have about two seconds to give her a hug and say 'Get on! There are thousands of people—go!' And she looks up at me and she goes, 'Have a good Easter, Dad. I'll see you tomorrow!'" This moment broke his heart, and it was a catalyst for change. He was tired of the large-scale production of ministry and the lack of personal mentorship. Yet even though he was cynical about what his church was doing, he was not done with being a pastor.

At this time, another—and even larger—megachurch approached him to be its lead youth pastor. This church consisted of a central campus with satellite congregations linked across the nation. It needed someone to develop small groups for the teenagers in its thirteen youth groups to make sure these ministries explicitly focused on discipleship. Marshall was intrigued by the prospect of a more spiritually focused youth group, and so he and his family moved across the country to lead the ministry.

As he began his work of forming small groups for the satellite churches, the central church asked him to be a speaker. He would film his sermons each week in an empty studio and broadcast them out to the youth groups during worship. He was a success with his broadcasted sermons. Teenagers loved him. They even asked him for his autograph when he would visit the satellite campuses! But this change created even more conflict and bitterness within him. His passion was developing relationships with teenagers, but he found himself alone in a recording studio every week. The result was a sense of alienation. He questioned if he should continue his job: "I'm kind of at the top of the game, and you'd be dumb to stop, but knowing that if I stayed in it, it could be at the cost of my soul—[*chuckle*] like I just would end up dying in this place and just becoming part of the system and scared of losing passion or whatever it may be. So I ran. I got out."

In order to "get out," Marshall and his family moved to Mexico to do mission work. The new ministry saw little pay and even less success than his previous work at megachurches. His mission work in Mexico fell apart, and he and his family moved back to the States after only a year.

Marshall is the one person in our study who was not looking to exit the ministry, but his story helps us understand how the role of a pastor can get in the way of one's calling. Even though he feels deeply frustrated by the pastoral role, he says, "I'm addicted to doing ministry." Yet he knew at that time that he would have to do something drastically different. As he describes it, doing ministry as he had previously done it was "not healthy for my soul." He and his wife planted a new, smaller, and less bureaucratic church in a western state. It is much smaller and slower. He describes his life now in much different terms: "I'm alive. I'm loving it—we're both loving it. We're doing it at a pace that's healthy for our souls."

ALIENATION, MARX, AND HOCHSCHILD

There is irony in Marshall's story. He became disconnected from the very thing he wanted to cultivate: a person's relationship with God. He wanted to nurture others' spiritual relationships, yet he ended up producing worship services, broadcasting sermons, and managing parking lots. The very thing he was passionate about—connecting souls with God—ended up being the aspect of ministry he spent the least amount of his time and energy working on.

Surprisingly, Marshall's story connects with the Industrial Revolution, over two hundred years ago. The Industrial

Revolution drastically changed where and how people worked. Instead of working on farms or in artisan workshops, more and more people labored in factories, where the hours were long and the work monotonous and often dangerous. Karl Marx, a social theorist during this time, was deeply concerned with the welfare of the working person. Marx noticed that workers in industrial factories become alienated, or disconnected, from what they produce and how they produce it.[1] Factory workers use their physical bodies to do their work, and in return, they receive wages. For Marx, this means that the workers' bodies actually become commodities that are bought and sold. The physical work these people perform in their jobs is not an expression of creativity or passion but simply labor performed in exchange for wages. In this system, it barely matters to the worker, or the employer, what work is being done. It only matters that an agreement can be reached to produce a particular quantity of goods for a sufficient wage. Marx succinctly describes the situation by saying, "The worker sinks to the level of a commodity."[2]

Marx also points out that workers are alienated from what they produce. Whatever the laborer makes in the factory is not his creation that comes from a deep expression of his inner being. Historically, an artisan chair maker would craft a chair from start to finish. When it was completed, he could use the chair or sell it, but it was his. With the beginning of factory work in the Industrial Revolution, workers no longer owned the products they created. Products became mere commodities to be sold in a marketplace. Marx states that this separation between the worker and his products is also a type of alienation.

An act that is at the core of what it means to be human—the act of creating—is reduced to toil when it must be used to create a product for wages. By using his body for many hours through many repetitions in a factory, Marx's worker is alienated from his own body because it is now a tool for economic survival and no longer a means through which he expresses his humanity in joyful and creative ways.

The resulting alienation is a loss of humanity for laborers. They perform their work because it earns them a wage and not because it is an expression of their own selves. The objects they create are no longer their own but only commodities sold for profit. Marx writes that under these conditions, "labour is *external* to the worker, i.e., it does not belong to his essential being; that in his work, therefore, he does not affirm himself but denies himself, does not feel content but unhappy, does not develop freely his physical and mental energy but mortifies his body and ruins his mind. . . . [The worker] is at home when he is not working and when he is working, he is not at home."[3] The physically demanding and often monotonous actions that workers use in factories to produce their wares dull their senses and creativity, diminishing what it means to be human, to be alive. Given this, it is no surprise that Marshall uses the term *alive* to characterize his new endeavor—outside of the days of factorylike ministry production that characterized his early pastoral career.

Arlie Hochschild, a sociologist, takes Marx's understanding of labor and alienation and applies it to contexts outside of the factory. According to her, *anything* that is used in the capitalist marketplace for one's job can be separated from a person. She writes, "The worker can become estranged or alienated from an aspect of self—either the body or the margins of the soul—that is *used* to do the work."[4] She uses the examples of flight attendants and bill collectors to show that they must produce emotions as a part of their jobs. Flight attendants create positive emotional environments to put their passengers at ease, while bill collectors generate negative emotions to motivate their clients to pay their debts. Emotions, for these two groups, become commodities that are produced and consumed in the marketplace.

Hochschild points out that, just as Marx's factory workers do with their own bodies and physical labor, flight attendants and bill collectors must mentally detach themselves from their own emotions in order to survive. The cost of labor in a capitalistic society is that workers are at the risk of losing their own capacities when they use these capacities to produce their products, whether they are physical, emotional, or in our sample, spiritual. When a flight attendant uses a personal emotional response—like a smile—in a public and economic manner, she loses the connection between smiling and authentic experiences. Smiling is part of her job description, and the display of emotional warmth is the product she is selling. As a result, the flight attendant is now alienated from her smile. She displays her smile, not because it is a genuine response to a positive emotion, but because she is economically obligated to provide a welcoming environment to her passengers.

Hochschild calls this process of using a private and personal experience as a commodity "transmutation."[5] Private, unconscious feelings are transmuted into something altogether different once they are used by large, impersonal organizations that sell commercial products. The process of transmutation leads to a separation of the "true self" from the "false self" for the worker.[6] Once a worker transmutes private emotions into a public, for-profit act, those emotions are no longer the worker's; they are the organization's. This creates a division between what one feels as a voluntary, personal response to life (the true self) and a produced emotion that is required as a part of one's job (the false self). The more a person offers her or his own true self to a job, the more that "self risks seeming false to the individual worker, and the more difficult it becomes for him or her to know which territory of self to claim."[7] As a result, emotion workers often disconnect from the very abilities they use in their jobs. These emotional capacities transmute from natural expressions into manufactured outputs.

Because people who use their emotions in their jobs often lose the capacities they use in creating their products, authenticity becomes a rare and precious phenomenon. As Hochschild succinctly puts it, "The more the heart is managed, the more we value the unmanaged heart."[8] In other words, a waitress who is required to be friendly in her job learns to cherish moments of unprompted, genuine friendliness from both herself and others. Yet even as spontaneous emotional reactions become valued and sought-after occasions, they are also examined by the alienated person with a certain amount of suspicion. People using their emotions for their jobs question whether their responses are products of a managed heart or truly expressions of their true selves.

PRODUCING A SPIRITUAL PRODUCT

Clergy use their own faith in their work nurturing and guiding their communities. They preach, lead worship, counsel, study, and manage congregations. Furthermore, pastors get paid to do so within the context of churches shaped by social Darwinism and capitalism. Congregations must compete with one another for people and money in order to survive. The winning congregations grow and keep their doors open, while the losers shut down.[9]

This puts profound competitive pressure on clergy to perform well. On the one hand, this "survival of the fittest" pressure ensures that people leading churches function at the highest level because if they don't, they are out of their jobs. On the other hand, it means that, like the flight attendant's smile or the factory worker's body, the clergy's *own faith* can become a commodity. The result is that, as Marx and Hochschild reveal, a pastor competing in the religious marketplace has the potential to become alienated from his or her own faith.

Someone's relationship with God comes from a very personal place, deep within them. Yet if Marx and Hochschild are correct, this very thing can be transmuted into a commodity that is used to perform a job in return for wages. Like a theme park employee's friendliness, a pastor's own personal relationship with God becomes a job requirement to be performed whether or not there is an authentic feeling behind it.

The pastors in our study provide evidence that spiritual alienation is not simply theoretical conjecture but an active reality for many clergy. These leaders find connecting with their own faith difficult because they are in charge of "producing" it for others. First, many of the pastors we spoke to are acutely aware that their ministry requires them to create a spiritual product for their congregants' consumption. Even though it was a spiritual product, it was nonetheless a commodity that needed to be excellent in order for their congregations to survive. Thomas, a thirty-eight-year-old former Baptist pastor, deeply understands how his performance as a pastor is connected to keeping his job, and he explicitly uses the language of manufacturing. He says, "Your portrayal of your humanity is your job security, right? If you can't manufacture an experience, you lose your job."

Adam, thirty-seven, also felt this pressure to produce when he was in the pastorate. He is a former nondenominational youth pastor at a large church in a western state. The leaders of his church approached him because they were disappointed in him. His youth ministry had a regular attendance of *only* one hundred students, but the leaders set a target goal of two hundred students. Adam was frustrated by this. He felt the most powerful spiritual moments he had when leading his group were when fifteen or twenty teenagers attended instead of the normal hundred. He describes this ideal situation: "So it was cool to be able to sit down to really impact these kids in a major way. . . . We'd get done with a youth group night, and I'd walk away and tell my wife, 'Man! Like that was awesome! You know, we only had fifteen kids, but these kids really had some awesome work done this evening!'" Adam says that after evenings like this, when there were lower numbers but profound spiritual experiences, his leaders in the next church staff meeting would reprimand him for not having more in attendance. He reports they would tell him, "You know, there were fifteen in the youth group. What's going on? You need to get those numbers up! You need to advertise more!" As a response, he felt the pressure to put on more extravagant youth meetings to attract more teenagers. As he did this, he felt like he maintained his integrity, but it was a struggle for him. He says, "We had different games and activities to attract the kids, and I never felt like I was being not authentic. But I was acting out of desperation because I knew I needed to maintain a certain level of production within my ministry."

Adam uses the explicit language of *production*, which recalls both factory labor and the theater. He felt the tension between being spiritually authentic and producing a show for the entertainment of his crowd. Yet he also felt disingenuous, like he was fabricating or producing so that his congregation could compete in the marketplace for teenagers' attention. He even describes his worship services in explicitly factory-oriented language. He says of his job, "Everything is manufactured in so many ways. I remember during our summer, we had some people on vacation. We pulled chairs out from the auditorium so that it made it look fuller in the service." Adam left his position at the large church, but he still feels called to be a spiritual leader. He's wrestling with how to lead others spiritually outside the traditional congregational context, so he is currently pursuing a master's degree in recreation with the hope of working for governmental or nonprofit agencies.

Jeff, thirty-five, is in a context remarkably different from Adam's, but he is feeling the same pressure to produce a product. He was an American Baptist pastor in the Northeast. After pastoring two small and failing congregations, he recently resigned out of frustration. He originally thought his calling was to be a worship leader. After studying music for a while in college, he realized "that music could manipulate people and that we could do this, and maybe it would feel like they were having a worship experience. . . . It's a manipulation of emotions and things in order to produce a quasi-spiritual experience." Jeff did not go into the music ministry but instead decided to be a pastor. Yet he continues to struggle with the relationship between being a spiritual leader and being in front of people leading worship. He says, "So there's an element of worship in which you're doing theatrics. You're a stage presence. You're an actor. It's very much, in the classical Greek sense, providing a catharsis for a group of people."

THE ALIENATION OF FAITH

Jeff has the sense that being a worship leader and being a spiritually authentic person can actually conflict. He goes on to say, "But you're trying to do it [lead worship] in a way that doesn't, you know [stumbles for words] . . . it doesn't diminish your own personal—like, that's the struggle. It's to not lose yourself in the process." Jeff's struggle to fully articulate his feelings is telling. It highlights the fact that the pastors we spoke to often feel a sense of alienation or separation from their own faith. When we ask Jeff to explain more about his struggles to "not lose yourself in the process," he says, "I'm afraid if I share too much of myself, then, you know, I'll overwhelm everybody." His fear is that if he shows his authentic relationship with God to his congregation, it will get in the way of his ability to be a good pastor. The conflict among the desire to be authentic with his congregation, maintain his own spirituality, and nurture others in their faith was too much. He resigned from his position as a pastor, was unemployed at the time of our interview, and frankly told us, "Pastoring is the most soul-killing job there is."

Similarly, Peter, sixty-two, was having trouble enjoying authentic spiritual experiences within the context of worship. He was on staff as a pastor in a large congregation affiliated with the Evangelical Covenant Church. He describes getting up on Sunday mornings as "depressing." Even though his congregation was large and bustling with energy, he felt the services in which he preached and the ministries he led were troubling. He says, "It just wasn't authentic. It wasn't real transformation. It was a job." In this "job," Peter would work during the week preparing for services on Sunday, but he felt isolated and trapped. He says, "It was something we spent the whole week preparing sequestered within the building and not engaged with the rest of the world, where Jesus wants us to be, to act out or teach kingdom principles. We were penned up. Penned up inside for what? To make sure the one hour or more is perfect."

This idea of creating perfection affected his family life as well. He tells the story of one Sunday morning driving to church with his wife and children. They were in a large fight, but when the car pulled into the parking lot, he told his family,

"All right! We've got to stop the fight right now!" For him, the image of the pastor's family fighting was incompatible with the image of being a pastor. His wife later told him, "When you walk into church, you start using the 'F' word." When he asked her what she meant by this, she replied, "When people ask you 'How are you today?' you always reply 'I'm fine.'" He felt like he was not able to go beyond "fine" in conversations with his congregants.

This struggle over image, what he calls "pretense," affected his faith. He says, "Pretense retards transformation because it discourages authenticity." The pressure to project a certain facade actually impeded the very core work of being a pastor—spiritual transformation. Peter struggled with being authentic with his congregants for two reasons. First, he was fearful of what they would think of him if he let them see his true self. He says, "I mean, if you're frustrated or down, then you really can't share that with someone. . . . You can't break below the surface to discover brokenness, the need to be healed, and the new life needed to take over."

The second reason Peter struggled with being authentic was that the members of his congregation expected an excellently performed Sunday worship experience. He delivered his sermons on a stage with lighting, directing cues, and even a haze machine. This limited what he could and could not do on stage in front of people. He describes one time when he was preaching. Someone had placed surgical tape underneath the microphone to mark where he should stand, and a spotlight lit up this area of the stage. During the sermon, he moved away from his mark and walked over to the side of the stage to make a teaching point with someone sitting in the front row. The entire stage crew waved to him from their tech booth in the back of the worship space. "Get back into the spotlight!" they silently yelled as they motioned for him to move.

He said this example was symbolic of the larger problem. He was not able to do what he felt came naturally—to connect authentically with people to nurture their faith.

Peter eventually left his position as a pastor and is now managing storage facilities. He feels this change has led him to be more authentic. He says, "I'm the happiest I've ever been. I can go on Facebook. I can talk with you [*the interviewer*]. I can share with people when they ask questions about the Bible, and I can tell them what I really think. . . . That to me is liberation."

THE SEARCH FOR AUTHENTICITY

Authenticity is critical for well-being, particularly in the workplace. When people act authentically in their lives, not only are they happier with their careers, but they also experience a deeper level of meaning in their work.[10] Authenticity can be described as "the ability of an individual to act according to his or her true feelings, beliefs, and core values."[11] When someone experiences something that is not authentic, there is a disconnect between external actions and internal emotions.

Peter's story highlights this disconnect, and many other pastors recounted similar experiences. Authenticity becomes increasingly rare because the pastors have to use their faith as a part of their job. They feel obligated to have a strong relationship with God, to be enthusiastic in worship, or to be prayerful. Pastors have their own personal and spiritual struggles, yet they often do not feel like they can be open about them because it would hamper their leadership of their congregations. As a result, their personal faith becomes "transmuted" and no longer flows from the pastor's core. It is a commodity that is *used*. As Jeff confessed earlier, he was worried that if he shared too much of his authentic self with his congregation, he would "overwhelm everybody."

Psychologists often break down authenticity into three components: thinking, living, and relating authentically.[12] To *think authentically* is to connect how one is feeling with one's awareness of those feelings. To *live authentically* is to act "in accordance with one's values and beliefs."[13] Finally, to *relate authentically* is to behave according to one's values even if others have different expectations. So with all three components combined, an authentic person (1) knows what they are feeling, (2) acts according to their own values, (3) and acts from their own desires and not necessarily because they want to conform to others' wishes.

The clergy we spoke to struggle with the last two dynamics of authenticity (living and relating authentically). They were able to think authentically. They were very aware of their emotions and values, but they were afraid to express them. There was a disconnect between what the pastors were feeling internally and what they actually did. In worship, they acted engaged, but internally, they were not feeling a deep spiritual connection with God. Likewise, these clergy often thought about how their congregants perceived them and sought to conform to others' social expectations, setting aside their own desires.

Nancy, a sixty-seven-year-old rector of a small Episcopal church in a western state, struggles with this aspect of authenticity in ways that echo both Peter and Jeff above. She is reluctant to be fully authentic with her congregation for fear of what they may think of her. She says, "People expect you to be the pastor all the time, and everybody has a picture in their mind of what a pastor is. If you don't fit that picture of what a pastor is, then you're clearly not a good pastor. So there is always a level at which I'm wondering how fully I can share myself and my humanity because of a sense of judgment. . . . It's difficult to share your own doubts and fears because people count on you to have the answer." Nancy is confronted with the dynamic of being an individual, a practicing Christian, and a priest who leads a spiritual community. To be an authentic, doubting, fearing, struggling person may not be in line with others' expectations of her role as a pastor. She feels that her parishioners may not be open to a leader who expresses those insecurities. As a result, Nancy feels the need to conceal her authentic self.

Charles, forty-five, was a pastor in the Presbyterian Church (U.S.A.), and he also wrestled with how to be authentic and be a pastor. On the surface, he was in a great position. He was a young associate pastor with a beautiful family in a wealthy community. He admitted that he "had it made" but struggled with being himself with his congregation. He says, "There is the dynamic that you can't be yourself. You've got to be a superior person. You can't smoke. You can't cuss. . . . But you have to be this morally superior person, and that's a really bad dynamic." He describes the pressure to be perfect as "unhealthy," and the lack of authenticity in his life led to some unhealthy outcomes. Charles says that he became depressed, gained weight, and then began drinking heavily during the day regularly. His marriage deteriorated during this time, which led to a divorce a few years later. He finally could not cope with the lack of authenticity he felt in his job, and he quit. He thought about serving in another church, but the pressure to be someone he was not as a pastor was too much. He is now a probation officer, a job that he loves because he can be himself and continue to help those in need.

Unlike Charles, Michael has yet to find a new career. As a thirty-five-year-old associate pastor with the Mennonite

Church Canada, Michael is actively looking for a change. He thinks many expectations are placed upon pastors, and it can be exhausting. The strongest expectation is to be "a perfect example." He says, "When I get affirmations, it's because others perceive me to be perfect. . . . I'm not sure how people would respond to me if I were frustrated or angry." He goes on to describe how pastors are not free to share with their congregations or say, "I am a broken person. I'm an alcoholic. Or I'm into drugs." To share these struggles would mean that he is no longer perfect, which would not live up to the expectations of his congregation.

According to Michael, this inability to be an authentic, complicated person can actually diminish a pastor's humanity. He says, "Some of those core realities or vulnerabilities of the human experience might be significantly muted for pastors because of the expectations that people have of them." He has not ruled out pastoral work altogether, but he feels as though something has to change so he can be his authentic self. His sense that the essential parts of being human are "muted" by being a pastor is exactly what Marx and Hochschild predict. He thought he had to project a version of himself that was "perfect" in order to fulfill his role as a pastor. To seem perfect, he believed, was a job requirement, and he feared that being less than perfect could have led to him losing his job. This lack of authenticity led him to a sense of alienation and separation from his core self. His complex human nature was reduced to a muted—although seemingly perfect—image.

A CHANGE IN FAITH

A few pastors we interviewed connected their struggle with authenticity to their changing faith. When we started this project, one of our first hypotheses was that the clergy who want to leave the church do so because of a *loss* of faith. Essentially, it is the secularization thesis repackaged for pastors. If more and more people are saying they are religious nones (i.e., they do not affiliate with any faith), then the movement away from faith must also affect religious leaders.[14] We did not find much evidence for pastors becoming nones and abandoning their faith. (Only Brian, whom we discuss in chapter 6, considers himself now a none.) What we did find, however, was that some of our pastors felt like their faith had moved beyond the confines of traditional, orthodox Christianity and that they could no longer be authentic and fake being orthodox.

Jared, thirty-four, is a bivocational youth pastor in a Southern Baptist church in a western state. He and Brian are the two pastors we spoke to who came closest to the traditional concept of "losing one's faith." After graduating from seminary with his MDiv and beginning his work in the local church, Jared began to notice a change in his faith. He says, "You know, my personal beliefs are really evolving and changing, and I'm having trouble staying just even in the denomination. I'm not sure my faith really is lining up with my career choice right now. That's an interesting place to be." His career is exhausting, and he describes it as being "stretched thin." Because he is bivocational, he works as a part-time teacher at the local private school. At his church, he leads youth group meetings on Sunday mornings, Sunday nights, and Wednesday evenings. After his church's music minister left, he picked up leading the church's worship service. However, there was no increase in pay for this additional work.

Yet at the core of Jared's distress is not his packed schedule or sparse pay. It's his changing faith. He says he's "asking a lot of questions" about what he believes, especially on issues like heaven, hell, and homosexuality. He says that this questioning stirs up a lot of fear within him because "you're kind of paid to be the guy who talks to God all the time." When we ask him why his questions bring about fear, he hesitates and speaks to us slowly, like he is critically thinking about every word. He carefully says, "The direction that I feel like I'm going is that there are days that it seems that I have no faith. There are days that I'm—I'm not entirely sure that I even believe in God. [*long pause*] And that's kind of the crux of everything."

Jared is paid to be the person who connects with God, and yet he is questioning the basic premise of this idea: God. He knows this is not great for his ministry. As he describes it, "I'm not in a place where I can actually be of a lot of help to people. . . . I'm stretched thin, and it's got to change." In his struggles with his faith and his career, he feels isolated. His entire social life revolves around the church, and his large extended family is deeply religious. He wonders, "Do I just have to get to a point and suck it up for the family? I don't know." Currently, he continues to serve in his church but is looking at going back to college to get a degree in engineering.

Similarly, Amanda, thirty-four, is an Episcopal priest in the South who struggles with being completely honest about her faith with others in her church. She is a very spiritual person with deep religious practices, but over time, she has begun to incorporate Native American spirituality with her Anglicanism. She says Morning Prayer from the Book of Common Prayer, but she also drums up the sun in the morning, calls for help from the Four Directions, and burns sacred herbs for cleansing. She has a home altar filled with traditional Anglo-Catholic items, such as an icon of the Virgin Mary. Yet she added a goddess statue that a friend gave her and a feather from a hawk, which she says is her spirit animal.

She struggles with the tension of being a very spiritual person and being an ordained leader within the Episcopal

Church. She says, "If I were to stand in front of the church and be completely honest, a lot of people would not say I am a Christian." She self-defines as Christian because she still believes that "Jesus is the Son of God, and he's a really important part of my life." However, she also views her spirituality as leading her beyond the walls of the church. She describes herself as a "person who is in touch with the Spirit and who sees God working not just in the church and not just through the people of the church but through the world, through creation." She feels as though she cannot fully express her spirituality with her bishops or denominational leaders. She says, "I think it's hard to be able to name authentically who you are as a pastor and your faith practices if they don't look exactly the way our churches describe they should look like." As a result, she left her position as an assistant rector and works full time at a bank while filling in on weekends for parishes that need a substitute priest.

CONCLUSION

The pastors we spoke to are struggling. They entered into this profession because of their desire and commitment to lead others toward God. Yet because they are paid to do so, their faith is transformed into a commodity they use to earn a salary. They are trying to balance having a deep, authentic life of faith with the pressures of being spiritual leaders in a competitive religious marketplace, one where congregations that do not perform close down or lose relevance.

Capitalism, for all its strengths and weaknesses, saturates North American Christianity. Religious practice and faith are produced within a marketplace with buyers and sellers. Churches are the "sellers," and the congregants, or "buyers," can easily walk out of one church and attend another the next week if they are not happy. Of course, this idea of buyers and sellers is not quite that transactional or rationalized, as the research about church switching has shown conclusively, but the existence of this basic dynamic pushes pastors to use their faith as a commodity.[15] They must create a spiritual product that is competitive with that of other churches in order to survive. The "product" may be excellent. It may be beautiful and meaningful for the church members. However, there is a cost, and the pastors who spoke to us say the cost is authenticity. It is difficult for these leaders to be both pastors and individual Christians whose spiritual lives may not be consistent with the traditional image of "pastor." They wrestle with how much of their authentic selves they can reveal before it diminishes their capacity to lead their congregations. Leading meaningful worship experiences challenges them because they "see how the sausage is made."

In many ways, the role of a pastor is getting in the way of being spiritual leaders for these ministers. Yet at the heart of their stories is their sense of a divine calling. These pastors believe they have been called by God to lead and to serve. This sense of calling is strong, but given how the pastoral role can hinder spiritual development, many have had to renegotiate what living out a calling looks like. This renegotiation of a divine calling is the topic we will explore in the next chapter.

THE TAKEAWAY

- North American congregations operate within the capitalistic marketplace, which means they are selling a product to consumers.
- Pastors can be alienated from their faith because they use it for their job as spiritual leaders.

- As a result, pastors can struggle with being authentic in their spiritual lives.

FOR REFLECTION AND DISCUSSION

For Pastors

- Do you ever feel a disconnect between the "official" faith you present to your congregation and your own personal faith? If so, how does that affect your ministry?
- Do you struggle with being authentic with your congregation? Do you think you are allowed to reveal your "true self," or do you think there would be negative consequences if you did?
- How can pastors lead worship and at the same time meaningfully participate in worship?

For Churches, Seminaries, and Denominations

- In your organization, are there unspoken pressures on pastors to act, live, or speak a certain way that might restrict how they express their authentic spiritual lives?
- What are some ways we can structure congregational life so that pastors are not "selling" their faith to recruit "consumers" of faith?
- How can you support pastors in being authentic in their spirituality?

CHAPTER 2
REDEFINING A CALLING

Being a pastor—the worst of all jobs and the
best of all callings.
—John Newton, nineteenth-century
Anglican priest[1]

Christopher, a banker-turned-Lutheran pastor, feels a strong
sense of calling, even as he is struggling to find a full-time pastoral position that will help support his family. Before he began
seminary, this call was affirmed by multiple people telling him
that they had always seen him as a pastor-like figure. He says,
"I knew the Holy Spirit was calling me in this direction. So
I was open to it. Things fell into place relatively quickly." Yet
while his entry into the ministry happened rather smoothly,
his remaining there has been quite difficult. Because his current pastoral job cannot pay a full salary according to denominational guidelines, he has become a substitute teacher, and
his wife has moved with the children 120 miles away to take
another job.

As a bivocational pastor who is involuntarily separated
from his family, Christopher is brainstorming *any* route to

make his calling within a congregation happen. He is considering becoming a permanent bivocational pastor. He says, "My biggest question now is, If I have to become bivocational, in what ways can I do this?" He has considered working as a tax preparer, drawing on his background in banking, but the peak tax season and the Lenten-Easter season overlap. He does not think that would be workable. He likes teaching but does not know which subject he could teach. He asks out loud in our interview, "So there's this frustration of what type of work can I do in correlation with ministry, *if ministry can't sustain me?*" (emphasis added).

The last part of Christopher's statement is important. Yes, he feels a strong sense of calling, so much so that he is willing to sacrifice a lot to be a pastor. His wife and children have moved to another town for work while he remains behind; he works in a part-time, low-paying position in the public schools; and he is actively considering making this a permanent situation. Yet he is losing faith that ordained ministry will work out. He has looked for other congregational positions. Most of those job postings are for similarly small congregations that cannot support a full-time pastor. Therefore, he believes the current way we've structured denominations, churches, and clergy is broken because it is not able to sustain the professional, full-time pastorate. This puts him in a precarious situation for living out his calling.

Like Christopher, the pastors in this study are frustrated. They are alienated from their own faith. They feel as though they are creating a product to be sold in the spiritual marketplace. Some have left the ministry, while others do not feel like they can leave—themes that we will explore in the upcoming chapters. Whether these pastors intended to continue in or leave ordained ministry, we asked each person if they still felt a calling from God. Before we began this project, we expected that we would hear pastors describe how they lost their sense of calling and that this shift was why they felt so dissatisfied with the ministry. This would be the secularization theory retold in terms of an individual's spiritual calling: North America is experiencing the loss of religion, and we can see this in pastors' no longer feeling a sense of calling.

This is not what we heard. Instead, one of the biggest surprises of our study was that these pastors answered the question "Do you still have a calling?" with a resounding yes. However, there was always a follow-up to this yes. Yes, these pastors felt a strong sense of calling from God, but they often told us that congregational ministry is no longer the location where they could fulfill this calling. Like Christopher, many wonder if the congregation may actually get in the way of their following God's call.

These pastors' certainty about their calling to ordained ministry reflects national survey data on clergy. In a 2001 nationally random survey, 62 percent of clergy never doubted their calling. This certainty increased to 73 percent in 2009 (table 2.1). The pastors in our study, however, nuanced their affirmation of their calling with a major caveat, usually about the *structure* of ministry. Many no longer felt that their calling could be carried out within the congregational form. As a result, they had to redefine their sense of calling from God.

THE POWER OF A CALLING

Ordained ministry is not only a profession; it is also a calling.[2] Of course, people other than clergy feel a calling to their work, but it is within the context of serving as a pastor that the word *calling* becomes synonymous with the word *career*. As H. Richard Niebuhr describes, there are different aspects to a pastor's calling.[3] Clergy are called by their communities

Table 2.1: Pastors who have doubted their calling over the past five years

	2001	2009
Very often	4%	1%
Fairly often	4%	4%
Once in a while	31%	23%
Never	62%	73%
N	*880*	*679*

Sources: Pulpit and Pew National Survey of Pastoral Leaders (2001) and US Congregational Life Survey (2008/9).
Data are weighted to account for congregational size.

(like Christopher experienced within his congregation). But clergy also experience a powerful, internal feeling, what Niebuhr calls a "secret call," when a person "feels himself directly summoned or invited by God."[4] Because it is so personal and intimately connected to the Divine, the concept of calling is powerful. A calling drives someone to serve others or God. It motivates a person to endure hardships and look beyond themselves to seek a higher purpose, just as Christopher and his family did when his wife and children moved away in search of other jobs. It also infuses a person's work with meaning and can transform that work to make it "morally inseparable from his or her life."[5] Therefore, people with a strong sense of calling—both laity and clergy—are more satisfied with their lives and their work, and they are less likely to suffer from depression and stress.[6]

And yet there is a dark side to a calling that people often do not acknowledge. Some describe having a calling as both "binding and ennobling."[7] It can lift people up to the highest levels of human potential. It can motivate them to do amazing things with their lives, giving them purpose and a sense of service to society or God. Yet it can bind people to a specific role. People who feel bound to their work are more at risk to be exploited by their employers because it is assumed they are doing the work for intrinsic rewards and not just for the money. They are more willing to work longer hours for less money and neglect their personal well-being in pursuit of this calling.[8] Also, people with a strong sense of calling may suffer from a sense of "tunnel vision" in their careers and become so focused on one path that they miss other excellent opportunities.[9] A sense of calling in a career, especially if it has religious connotations, can lock a person into that career, even if they want to leave. As a pastor friend of ours tells us, "Nobody fears for their eternal soul when they leave their law firm, but leaving a job you felt called to by God is quite another thing."

Christopher's life exemplifies this dual nature of calling. His career is ennobling because he is a spiritual leader within his community, serving others in the name of God. But his calling has been a binding force on him so that he is separated from his family and struggling with poverty. The other pastors in our study also struggle with this two-sided aspect of calling. As the quote at the beginning of the chapter indicates, being a pastor can be "the worst of all jobs and the best of all callings." It is absolutely a virtuous force for those who feel called, leading them to serve others for their faith. Yet their calling can also be an obstacle that hinders their lives. It limits opportunities or keeps pastors stuck in situations that are not ideal. Some pastors struggle because the organizations to which they are called are themselves unsustainable as institutions. They must balance the grand idea of a calling with the reality of limited (and often diminishing) resources. Others we interviewed have had to redefine their calling. To serve as an ordained clergy person was no longer a viable option, and yet they experienced a transcendent call to do so. In order for their calling to continue to be a positive power, they had to change their understandings of what it entails. In fact, one of the distinguishing features of pastors who did not feel stuck was their ability to successfully redefine their understandings of their calling and to acknowledge that it could at least potentially or hypothetically exist outside of the traditional congregational structure. Even the possibility of living out one's calling outside of the congregational model seemed to provide frustrated pastors with mental and spiritual assurance through difficult times.

I DON'T KNOW WHERE ELSE

Aaron, like Christopher, struggles with the relationship between his calling from God and that from the very institutions he expects to give his calling life. He sees his congregation as actually hindering spiritual development. He is a United Methodist pastor in a southern state. He has created "small groups" within his church to deepen his congregants' spirituality. He is frustrated because many of his parishioners have pushed back against the change. They do not want to adjust their church's schedule because the small groups conflict with the congregation's bingo game.

When we spoke to him, he was about to go through his last denominational interview in the ordination process to be an "elder in full connection" (an ordained minister) with the United Methodist Church. We asked him why he was about to go forward within the United Methodist denominational system, and he tied his calling to his theology and yet separated it from the larger structure of his church. He says, "Honestly, it's because I still feel called to ministry. And even if the Methodist Church falls apart or if something else happens down the road, my hope is that those credentials would be transferable in some way. . . . I really like the Wesleyan views on spirituality, on salvation and sanctification, on the lifelong process, on social justice—the whole works. I'm kind of stuck with that." For Aaron, his sense of calling to a life of Wesleyan spirituality is the driving force for his career as a pastor. This has led him to stick with a structure that, at times, has been antithetical to his calling as a spiritual leader. We asked him what his biggest frustration was, and he replied, "It's a combination of how I spend my time and the lack of response to deeper spiritual movements. There is this underlying expectation [from the congregation] that 'So long as you visit us and make us feel comfortable and loved, and you don't put us to sleep on Sunday morning with your sermon, then it will be good.'" His call is to lead the people in his church into deeper spiritual territory, but he struggles to do this within the context of his congregation. Yet he continues to serve within the system because the denominational-congregational system is often the only institution that focuses on spirituality and faith in North American religion.

We asked him why he does not change careers and leave ministry. He tells us, "I don't know where else to find that outlet to do the work that I feel called to do, and so I find these outlets in the small groups and in my writing. I just don't know where I can find another job that would allow me to invest the time in that piece [spirituality]." Aaron does not perceive any alternatives, and so he feels stuck. He is pursuing ordination in hopes that something will change but is doubtful that it will. He remains because he believes he is called.

REDEFINING A CALLING

While Aaron and Christopher are trying to live out their calling within the limits of the congregational system, other pastors are actively redefining their calling with themselves, although they are not congregational pastors. Since he left his job in a large congregation, Adam, the thirty-seven-year-old former youth pastor from chapter 1, has been struggling because youth ministry was always his career goal. He says, "I've always wanted to be a pastor, specifically a youth pastor. I knew that probably from the time I was seventeen years old." Although he is no longer in youth ministry, he continues to have a deep sense of calling. He says, "I feel like I'm called to be a spiritual leader in some capacity but not in the traditional sense. I just don't know really what that entails." He is enrolled in a master's degree program in recreation in hopes of working in a parks and recreation department for the government. We asked him if this transition felt like a violation of his calling, and he replied, "I think I redefined that aspect of calling. I feel like God still has a calling on my life, but I don't know what it is yet." This theme of continuing to sense a calling to ministry and not fully understanding how this calling will take place was common among the pastors who are no longer in congregational ministry. These pastors have had to reframe what calling means in order to continue serving without cognitive dissonance.

Jeff, the American Baptist pastor who recently resigned, is also redefining his calling. For him, authenticity is the foundation of his calling. As discussed in chapter 1, this means being able to share all aspects of his spiritual life with others. When his job within a congregation constrained his ability to be fully true to himself, he left. We asked him if he continued to feel a calling on his life. He says, "I would say I haven't given up on the concepts of ministry, but I would rather do it in a context where I'm free to share authentically who I am and not in a place where it's tied directly to my paycheck." Jeff has had to redefine his calling as something that is separate from the congregation. It is a calling not to the *career* of a pastor but instead to a lifestyle of living authentically and guiding others into deeper relationships with God. In redefining his calling, his understanding of church has also changed. He is still passionate about the church, but he says, "I don't necessarily really think that the church is dwindling. We just need to redefine what the church is and find out where it is." Like his calling, he has had to separate the idea of church from the institutional structures of congregations and denominations.

Charles, the former Presbyterian pastor who is now a probation officer, redefined his calling so that it included careers other than being a pastor in a congregation. The original calling that led him to seminary was "to work with hurting people." He thought that he could do that within the congregational context, and yet he was disappointed because he worked with only wealthy white suburbanites. We asked him why he did not change congregations, and he replied, "I didn't see any real difference." We wanted to know if he no longer felt called, and so we asked him, "Does the calling go away?" He says, "No, and that's why I am in a helping profession." For him, his work as a probation officer fits squarely within his calling to work with hurting people. He continues, "I definitely feel like why I'm here is to help people. I want to work in people's lives and try to give them some hope. But to do it in an institutional faith setting? No way!" For him, working outside of the congregational structure was a better way for him to fulfill his calling, which he had redefined to include a broader array of professions other than being a pastor.

Lisa too is done with the congregational structure, and so she has had to reframe what her calling means. She had a powerful and dramatic calling experience. She felt a calling to ministry early on but grew up in a Black Baptist tradition that discouraged women in ministry. She says, "So I pushed that calling aside because in my worldview as a child, my congregation was the church with the big 'C.' So if they didn't affirm me in that calling, then it really must not be a calling, or so I thought." She remained active in her church and continued to hear a calling from God to be a pastor.

As a lesbian, Lisa struggled to find a context where she could fully follow her calling and authentically live out her sexuality. She found and joined the United Church of Christ (UCC), a progressive denomination that valued her voice as a Black woman and lesbian. She describes this discovery: "I was excited to have found a denomination that accepted me in the totality of my being, and then to hear that call again was really affirming for me." She did not enter into ministry immediately. She had a career in the technology industry and volunteered at her church. One day, she was feeling down because of the difficulties in her tech job, and she had a profound spiritual experience. She describes,

> I was in my car leaving my job and feeling very unful-filled in that role. And I was having a conversation with God in the car, and God speaks to me. I hear God, but I know that's just me. But God said very clearly to me, "OK, you've done what you wanted to do. Now it's time to do what I called you to do." And that was everything to me at that moment. And it gave me the courage and the peace within myself to let go of that career because it was certainly more than a job at that point.

From this dramatic experience, Lisa left her career in technology, moved across the country, and entered seminary. She felt initially like she had just entered into a ministry that would last a lifetime. Yet things did not turn out as she planned.

She left her pastorate after her congregation was not comfortable with her involvement with social justice issues, a story we will examine in chapter 3. She could not follow her calling in a way that separated the gospel from social justice. When we asked her if she continued to feel a call, she offered the "Yes, but" answer. She told us yes, she does feel a calling, but she is unsure of the congregational structure. She says, "I don't look at the church the same way, but I know there is still a calling on my life to serve pastorally in a clergy role. But the context and the setting have not yet been revealed to me." She continues, "I want no part of pastoral ministry in the traditional setting. I can absolutely see maybe doing a church plant starting as a house church, a body that writes into the bylaws that we will never own property." Lisa has had to redefine her calling so that it includes being a spiritual leader outside of traditional congregations that own property. She is currently working back in the technology sector and is actively looking for creative ways to serve within the UCC.

THE CULTURAL TOOL KIT
FOR SPIRITUAL LEADERSHIP

The pastors we spoke to feel a strong sense of calling, and yet something is not working. The congregational structure often got in the way of faithfully serving as a pastor. For Christopher, the issue was that the church's dwindling resources could not support his call. For Jeff and Lisa, leading a congregation conflicted with their sense of authenticity and did not allow them to be truly themselves. Charles and Aaron felt like the congregation did not allow them to follow their calling to be *spiritual* leaders. In each case, the current structure of American religion—the congregation—thwarted their efforts to fully live out their calling.

Pastors are trying to follow their calling using the models that previous generations have handed down to them. If a person wants to be a spiritual leader, the cultural model in North America is for the person to serve as a pastor of a congregation.[10] (Yes, there are other venues in which to serve as a clergyperson, such as a chaplaincy, but these opportunities are the minority.[11])

The sociologist Ann Swidler uses the metaphor that culture can be viewed as a "tool kit."[12] When we want to do something, we reach into the tool kit provided by our culture to see what tools are available to choose from. For example, if we as North Americans wanted to advocate for a hot-button political issue—like gun ownership rights or a woman's right to an abortion—we would probably use the values of individualism and freedom to help support our claims. We might say something like "We are free as individuals to make our own choices." Sociologists would view "individualism" and "freedom" as the cultural tools our North American culture has given to us in our tool kit, and so those are the tools we pull out when we decide how to think about an issue.

One primary tool our culture offers for religious life is the congregational form. When we want to create a community that is focused on religious faith, we go to the congregation-as-voluntary-association model in North American culture. We see this most clearly in Buddhist or Hindu immigrants who come to Canada or the United States from cultures that do not use the congregational form in their religious lives. In their former countries, they never thought about their religion as having "congregations," but once they arrive in North

America, they often set up temples that resemble typical congregations with weekly meetings, professional clergy, and religious educational classes.[13] Similarly, the congregation is the tool that our culture offers for people who want to be spiritual leaders. When persons want to help people deepen their relationships with God or teach the Scriptures or lead in worship, one of the few avenues to do this is by working in congregations, often as pastors.

This congregational "tool," however, is no longer working for these people. To further the tool kit metaphor, it is like these pastors need to saw off something, but when looking into their tool kits, they only have hammers. The congregational structure either hinders deep spiritual development because it is so focused on institutional maintenance—like budgets, members, or even the colors of hymnals—or constrains leaders from full authenticity because pastors feel like they cannot share their true selves.

And yet because congregations are one of the few tools our society offers for developing a person's spiritual life, they are important. In her book *Sacred Stories, Spiritual Tribes*, sociologist Nancy Ammerman explores how people bring spiritual practices into their everyday lives.[14] Often our culture presents a narrative that spirituality and religion are at odds with each other. People can be "spiritual but not religious." They can have spiritual practices without being embedded in a religious community. Ammerman finds that this dichotomy is false. The most spiritually grounded people are the ones who are more active in their congregations, which she calls "sites where sacred consciousness is being socially created and sustained."[15] Ammerman writes, "When people do not have regular sites of interaction where spiritual discourse is a primary lingua franca, they are simply less likely to adopt elements of spirituality in their accounts of who they are and what they do with themselves. If they do not learn the language, it does not shape their way of being in the world."[16] In other words, religious congregations exist for a reason. They are the main cultural tools for cultivating spirituality and religious practice in North American society. Congregations are the major repository of spiritual and religious culture for many people.[17]

And so many pastors are caught in a paradox. The main tool our culture offers for spiritual leadership is not working for a lot of religious leaders. These clergy are called to be spiritual leaders, but they find that congregations can actually limit their capacity to provide spiritual leadership. When they search for other ways to be faith leaders, they do not find many other options. Some are working through their misgivings within the congregational model, like Aaron within the United Methodist Church. Some have left and are trying to fulfill their calling in other professions, like Charles as a probation officer. And others, like Lisa, are asking, "What comes next?" What other structures or forms can our culture create in order to give people routes to become spiritual leaders? The question, as of now, remains unanswered.

The task of finding an answer to this question is reaching a critical point. Within an environment of secularization and clergy abuse scandals, religious institutions are simply not in a place in 2022 to be running off good, talented, and called pastors. There may once have been a time when denominations and congregations could afford to lose a few bright and able professionals, but that time has passed. It is crucial that religious institutions begin to create the structures and forms necessary to expand the tool kit available and meet the challenges of the modern world.

THE TAKEAWAY

- Pastors feel a strong sense of calling to serve God and others, but many question if congregations are viable venues in which to live out this calling.
- A calling can have a dual nature. It can be an "ennobling" force in one's life, but it can also "bind" people so they do not pursue other, better opportunities.
- Some pastors have had to redefine their understandings of "calling" so they can fulfill their calling outside of congregations.
- Our culture offers one main tool—the congregation—for the place of spiritual leadership.
- People who want to be spiritual leaders outside of congregations lack viable options.

FOR REFLECTION AND DISCUSSION

For Pastors

- How has your calling been an "ennobling" force in your life? How has it been a "binding" one as well?
- In what ways does the congregational structure allow you to live out your calling?
- How do you feel that congregations get in the way of your fulfilling your calling?

For Churches, Seminaries, and Denominations

- What is your pastor's calling? Have you spoken to him or her about it recently? In what ways is your congregation supporting this call? How are you getting in the way of your pastor living out his or her calling?
- How do seminaries prepare their graduates for the *profession* of the clergy, and how do they prepare

people who live out the *concepts* of spiritual leadership regardless of their careers?

- What other forms exist within your denomination that allow people to follow a calling to be spiritual leaders? Are these forms sustainable?

PART II

STUCK IN THE CONGREGATION

CHAPTER 3
THE CONGREGATION AS BOTH A COMMUNITY OF FAITH AND A BUSINESS

Religion both needs most and suffers most from institutionalization.

—Thomas F. O'Dea and
J. Milton Yinger, "Five Dilemmas in
the Institutionalization of Religion"

Anthony, sixty-four, is one year from retirement, and it cannot come soon enough. Before he felt a call into the ministry, he worked in the federal government for twenty years. He left his job to begin seminary, became ordained, and began his twenty-three-year stint as a pastor in the United Methodist Church. Now, as a senior pastor in the Northeast, he is exhausted and frustrated, but he is quick to point out, "I'm not burned out." Unlike the pastors from the previous section who felt spiritually alienated from their faith because of their profession, Anthony's main frustration is *organizational*. He feels like the church is too business focused and not spiritual enough. He says, "I feel that the work I am doing as a local pastor is much more like being a manager of a small franchise than it is a deeply religious movement toward God."

As a United Methodist, Anthony's supervisor is his bishop, who has given each pastor "markers" that define success as a congregation. These markers include how many people attend worship, the number of people joining the congregation, the number of people in small groups, the amount of money given to missions, and whether the congregation pays its "apportionment" (the amount of money passed on to the denomination for missions, education, and administration). These metrics, which focus on quantity, frustrate Anthony. He says, "While I've always kept my fingers on those markers, those have been secondary to our primary purpose, which is to help people who come [to our church] to experience God." But for him, it is difficult to relegate the metrics to a secondary place. He thinks they are becoming the *focus* of ministry. He says, "That model has just taken over more of what this work is about and what churches are starting to look like. It's no longer a place I feel that I want to give that kind of heart, soul, and time that it requires. I want to . . . I *need* to step back from that."

He reports his bishop and other denominational leaders openly state they want the clergy in his denomination to transition from a pastoral-counselor model to an "MBA-entrepreneur model" that uses these markers of growth as indicators of success. He says this "church growth business model stuff" even affects how he interacts with other pastors. He says that many of his clergy friends wish they had gotten an MBA at business school instead of an MDiv at seminary. Other pastor friends describe their congregations not in terms of how they are doing spiritually but in terms of what percentage of their apportionments they paid to the larger denomination. Anthony is done with this business model of congregational life. He says, "This stuff, for me, is overshadowing what I would want to have as a congregation. . . . This is not something that I would desire to keep pouring myself into."

He is different from the pastors described in the previous section. He is not moving away from being a pastor because he feels alienated from his spiritual life. He does not feel as though he produces a product that is sold through his church. He has not had to redefine his calling. In fact, his spiritual life is quite robust. He takes spiritual retreats, and he loves corporate worship. He is done with being a pastor because it no longer feels like a *spiritual* profession. It is increasingly becoming a corporate profession, or as he says, "It is too driven by numbers."

CONGREGATIONS ARE DUAL NATURED

The tension between the spiritual side and the business side of congregations in Anthony's story demonstrates that a pastor's problems in the ministry are not always centered on a person's individual faith. They can reflect larger institutional problems that are beyond the control of local pastors. Cultural and demographic shifts in society can profoundly affect how pastors do their work, how others interpret pastoral work, and how pastors view their own profession.

Societal changes place immense institutional pressure on churches because congregations are dual natured. They are both spiritual and physical, transformational and transactional, and these two natures often pull congregations in two directions at once. On the one hand, congregations are *spiritual* entities and seek to offer places of worship and service to God. They are assemblies where people connect to God, pray, study Scripture, receive spiritual counseling, support one another, and serve their broader communities.

Yet on the other hand, North American congregations have never been solely spiritual organizations. They are also *physical* and *financial* entities. Because neither Canada nor the United States has a state religion supported by taxes, religious groups have always been aware that they must recruit enough members and raise enough money to survive. They need to maintain buildings. They must pay for heating and air-conditioning bills or have tables and chairs for events. Most congregations have staff who receive wages. Therefore, churches are more than just spiritual gatherings. They resemble a type of business, and if they are to stay open, they must generate resources—both members and money.[1] Pastors are caught between these dual natures. They must care for their flocks' spiritual lives, and yet they must also maintain the resources their congregations need to continue over time.

This survival-of-the-fittest social Darwinism is not new for North American religions. Since the colonial period, religious groups have had to grow their memberships or raise enough money to endure.[2] What has changed is that social Darwinism is now coupled with broad-scale secularization. With fewer resources now to gather, survival is not guaranteed for congregations. This has created a tension for pastors that has pushed them past the tipping point. Because church membership and attendance are declining, clergy have had to adopt practices that keep their congregations financially viable—practices that often get in the way of the spiritual purpose of the church.

THE BATTLE FOR LEGITIMACY

All organizations—and not just congregations—can be caught in a tug-of-war between two or more powerful forces. When a tug-of-war happens within any organization, it usually responds to the more culturally successful force, a process sociologists Paul DiMaggio and Walter Powell call "mimetic isomorphism."[3] Mimetic isomorphism means that groups copy—or mimic—other groups they deem to be more legitimate or successful than themselves. The concept of legitimacy is at the heart of the mimetic isomorphic process because groups want to be viewed as the cultural standards in their fields.[4] Organizations compete with one another for this powerful stamp of approval. As an example, in the field of higher education, the most legitimate (and therefore most prestigious) groups are the Ivy League schools of Harvard, Yale, and Princeton. Other universities copy their architecture, curricula, and culture in order to be seen as legitimate.

The battle for legitimacy takes place among congregations as well. For instance, when a large, successful congregation uses a rock band, strobe lights, and a smoke machine in its worship services, other churches are likely to follow this practice in order to be perceived as more legitimate. Congregations mimic one another's architecture, websites, and worship leaders' style of clothing so they can be accepted. Yet churches copy more than just other churches; they will also copy for-profit businesses—the most legitimate groups within a capitalistic environment. Their goals are to maximize profits (the goal of capitalism in general), become more efficient, and always be growing. These business practices become the churches' practices, and congregations begin to resemble companies.

Mimetic isomorphism is especially powerful when the social environment has an element of uncertainty within it.[5]

When a group is unsure about its success or its survivability, it is even more likely to look to other types of organizations to mimic. In the early twenty-first century, congregations are absolutely in a social environment of uncertainty. Worship attendance and church membership are down overall.[6] Even if a single, particular congregation is growing, it still operates within the larger, overall culture of declining attendance. As churches have struggled to keep membership up, they have turned their focus toward the business community to see how corporate strategies can help them survive. The thinking is that "the church needs to operate like a business." Businesses have succeeded financially, and so it makes sense for congregations to mimic their practices.

Copying a successful organization from another field is a good way to ensure survival in the short run. Yet these tactics often undermine the long-term success of the organization because these new practices may be at odds with the group's foundational, core purpose.[7] Congregations that adopt the business mindset of growth and efficiency may be more likely to survive in an environment of secularization. It is not necessarily a bad thing for congregations to want more members, especially given their commitments to evangelization. But they may also undermine their core commitments—to be communities of faith and mercy and to follow a crucified Christ. These goals often conflict with a growth mindset because they require sacrifice, humility, and generosity—postures rarely found in a business environment. Our stuck pastors feel this tension. Clergy have always had to be mindful of budgets and memberships, but the pastors we spoke to believed they were having to focus solely on managing resources at the expense of leading spiritual flocks.

THE NUMBERS GAME

One of the commonalities among businesses and churches is the desire for numerical growth. Many people see businesses as growing entities. New fast-food restaurants are springing up in neighborhoods, and technology companies, such as Google and Amazon, are expanding at a rapid pace. Compared to these developing businesses, many churches seem to be struggling. Yes, some individual congregations are growing, but overall, most churches have either plateaued or shrinking memberships.[8] Pastors are often held responsible for the softening numbers in worship. If a church is not growing, congregants often look to their leaders—and not to larger systemic issues, such as changing demographics or the growth of the nones—as the source of the problem. Therefore, the measuring stick of success for a pastor is often how many people are showing up in worship. In essence, a "good" pastor is one who leads a large church, and a "bad" pastor is one with a small congregation. The pastors in our sample suggested that this "numbers game" puts a lot of pressure on them to make sure there are people in the pews.

Nancy, the sixty-seven-year-old Episcopal priest who was fearful of being authentic with her parish from chapter 1, mentions struggling to keep an organization afloat while focusing on people's spiritual lives. Her church is small, and she directs a lot of her energy toward making sure the doors remain open. But this is not the focus she wants for her ministry. She says, "I'm much more interested in sustaining the relationships than sustaining the institution." Yet both her supervisors and her parishioners want more than growth in people's spiritual lives. They want growth in the number of people attending. She says, "They really wanted someone who grew the church, but it was frustrating for me because it's not really something a pastor can do a lot." For her, the numbers game feels out of her control. Too many other factors lead to a church having empty pews, like changing neighborhood demographics or national patterns of church attendance. Yet for Nancy, how people perceive her job performance is connected to making sure her church grows.

Even though he is in a remarkably different context from Nancy's, Stephen feels the same way. As a middle-aged, bivocational, evangelical pastor in the Midwest, Stephen leads a large satellite congregation that is an offshoot of another large church, and he owns a few business franchises. He says that often the focus of his church ministry is numerical growth and not spiritual growth, and he notices that many of his coworkers in his megachurch believe the ends of ministry often justify the means. He explains, "So if the auditorium is full, if people are being baptized, then the means [we used to get] there, the broken relationships, the poor leadership, the celebrity or CEO pastor, the questionable use of funds, all that kind of stuff pales in comparison to the fact that the church is full." He describes this mentality of doing anything, whether ethical or not, in order to fill the church as "unhealthy." In his large, successful ministry, everything revolves around the numbers game because people have defined success as being large.

A BUSINESS MODEL FOR PASTORAL LEADERSHIP

For Stephen, the numbers game is only a symptom of a larger, more disastrous problem eating away at the heart of the institutional church. He has a very high ecclesiology, or theology of the church. He says, "The church is here for a reason, has a mission, has a purpose." He continues to feel called to be a part of this mission. Yet he believes that the church has transitioned away from being a spiritual entity and toward becoming a business. He is quite familiar with the business world. He does not have a theological degree from a seminary, and he has not always been a pastor. Instead, he was (and continues to be) a very successful franchise owner. He was originally attracted to the ministry in an evangelical megachurch because it blended following Jesus with a businesslike efficiency. Reflecting back, he does not think this was the best model. He describes his entry into a pastoral role: "I think that's what probably attracted me initially in the wrong way to that larger church . . . because [it was] super business-like, very high on professionalism, very high on efficiency and effectiveness. That's kind of how I'm wired anyway, so I loved that part of it."

Now he says that because a business model of efficiency and effectiveness permeates American culture, pastors use this to run their churches. Using the same language of producing a product as the pastors from chapter 1, he says, "And maybe this was in the past seventy-five years of evangelicalism where we are producing a product: pray the prayer, check the box, raise your hand, go to the altar, whatever that number or metric is. There's a product to be driven. And so because of that, we tend to take on very businesslike applications to get that product. Having been still very much inside the business world and run businesses, I don't think it's the same. I think it's very different." For him, the church is not a business. It should not be run with only efficiency in mind. Businesses focus on profits and the generation of capital. Congregations do not have this focus. They are relational and spiritual organizations. And yet pastors are turning to the business world to shape their ministry. This, Stephen believes, is dysfunctional.

Amanda, the thirty-four-year-old Episcopal substitute priest and bank teller who connected Native American spirituality to her Anglican faith, also spoke up about how the business-model world crowded out the spiritual nature of her job. When she was a full-time priest, she was frustrated by the fact that she did not get to focus her time on working with her parishioners or nurturing others' faith. Instead, she became a glorified accountant and business manager. She says,

> What I became was somebody who crunched numbers and went to business meetings. I got to play with the kids on the weekends because I did the youth program, but the stuff that I thought I was going to do, the stuff I thought I was going to get paid to do, was not that. I thought I was going to get paid to be with people. I thought I was going to get paid to work in the world. . . . But in that situation, I felt like I didn't have space to do the pastoral work that I wanted to do because of the "number work" that I had to do.

For Amanda, this "number work" overshadowed the pastoral nature of her job as a priest.

Jeff, the recently resigned American Baptist pastor who described pastoring as the "most soul-killing job there is," explicitly states that the church has adapted to the business world for models of congregational leadership. He is very specific as to which particular business has influenced his church—Walmart. To him, it means "doing the same work for less money." A few years ago, his denominational leaders asked him to lead a congregation that was "on hospice." The church was dying, and they needed someone to oversee its closure. Jeff agreed that he would lead it for $300 a week plus living in a parsonage. After a few years, the church had not closed, but it had run out of money. Jeff continued to lead the church without pay. To help cover his expenses, he became the pastor of a second church, which also paid him $300 a week. Even this church was not able to pay him regularly. At one point, he went nine months without receiving a paycheck. He supplemented his meager income by officiating funerals for their honorariums. (He has conducted over 120 in the past few years.) He also spent all of his retirement savings keeping his family afloat financially so that he could pastor these two congregations. This situation was unsustainable. He says, "You invest yourself in the community. You invest yourself in the church. These people have to know that you are not pulling out, that you are not leaving, that you're here for the long haul. . . . And as we come to the five-year mark, we are completely out of resources." He and his family are "flat broke," and he describes his circumstances as "desperate."

Jeff is done—mentally, spiritually, and financially—with this situation. For him, this "Walmart approach" treats congregations as businesses that, to be profitable, must operate with the lowest costs possible. Clergy, as workers, are a cost and not a resource and therefore must be paid as little as possible. Jeff views the American Baptist Churches as operating with this mentality. He is frustrated that his denominational leaders expected him to serve these two congregations for so little pay. He says that the American Baptist Churches has the lowest clergy compensation guidelines out of all Mainline Protestant denominations. It also promotes bivocational pastors, which he describes by saying, "You can go get a job to work for somebody else to pay yourself to work for us."

In our interview with him, he was understandably angry and cynical. His recent experience quitting two ministerial jobs that did not pay him was quite fresh in his mind. He reflects back to how his denominational leaders treated the subordinate clergy using the business mindset: "What other job is there where both corporate and local managers, like the denominational leaders, conspire that you should work another job or pay yourself to work for them for less? That's the Walmart approach! [The denominational leaders say,] 'Hey, we can't afford you. Well, maybe we can. We'll make our labor force work for less!'"

THE IRON CAGE OF CONGREGATIONS

The ministerial experiences of Stephen, Amanda, and Jeff were different in some ways. Stephen worked in a giant Evangelical megachurch, while Jeff and Amanda served small Mainline congregations. And yet each of them felt that the business world had permeated their ministry, so the role of a pastor was transformed into that of someone working for a business. Amanda felt like an accountant crunching numbers. Jeff connected his ministry to a minimum wage worker, and Stephen's work was almost like a chief operations officer in a large corporation making sure that everything was done efficiently. For all three, this business mentality hindered their ministry with people. These pastors were less able to connect with and lead people spiritually because they had to focus on money and profit.

These pastors were struggling with the institutional pressures found in the numbers game and in the church-as-a-business model. They had to be efficient and cost-effective by keeping their memberships and revenues up while limiting their costs. Some told us they felt like they should have earned an MBA at business school instead of their MDiv at seminary.

Ultimately—and most striking—*many pastors felt like local congregations were no longer the places where ministry happens.* Lisa, a former United Church of Christ (UCC) pastor who is now working in information technology, describes why she left the ministry: "There was so much focus on the building and the bills and all of the upkeep that it takes to maintain the brick-and-mortar church. It seemed there wasn't much ministry being done." The actual day-to-day running of a congregation constrained these pastors so much they no longer felt like their work was spiritual or meaningful.

At the heart of this problem is a concept called "rationalization." Originally theorized by sociologist Max Weber, rationalization is the social force that pushes organizations toward bureaucratization, calculation, uniformity, and efficiency.[9] Rationalization transforms the ministry of leading people in their relationships with God into managing an organization with budgets, programming, and membership rolls. Pastors can see rationalization in their ministries when things become overly procedural and bureaucratic.

Weber understood that bureaucracies are powerful social creations. They can coordinate thousands of people through the use of hierarchies, rules, and regulations. They excel at accomplishing tasks efficiently. Noah, a fifty-three-year-old senior pastor of a Baptist church, spoke about how the bureaucratization of his congregation hinders his spiritual leadership: "You have your boards—the trustee board, the deacon board, and the committees—and you get together there, and it's about doing 'the business of the church.' And it seemed like the way we were doing church was providing a structure to keep an organization going, but there was never the time or the inclination to really share life in Christ." For Noah, the bureaucratization of his congregation was frustrating. He called the structure "safe and predictable and respectable," but he also said that it did not create "much cause to step out in faith and to really engage God or one another." Each Sunday, he found himself "becoming the least content person in the room as I'm standing up front leading worship and preaching." He struggled with whether to leave his pastoral ministry.

He felt called to serve these people, but the bureaucratization of his congregation was getting in the way.

Bureaucracies have a dark side. They can constrain individuality and freedom, and they often do not permit actions that are inefficient or that will change the status quo. Weber calls the negative side of the rationalization within bureaucracies "an iron cage."[10] Pastors feel this iron cage, and it is one of the main reasons for wanting to leave the local church. They have a passion for leading others spiritually—or as Noah puts it, "to really share life in Christ." They feel called to work with people in some of the deepest aspects of their lives: births, deaths, marriages, doubts, and faith. Many go to seminary to ground this calling with a strong academic foundation. Yet once they begin to work in congregations, they realize much of their job is not spiritual leadership. It is maintaining a rationalized, bureaucratic organization. This rationalization restrains these pastors from being the ministers they were called to be. Instead of focusing on people, they must focus on budgets. Instead of challenging their congregations to draw deeper to God, they must focus on making sure they are attracting enough members. These congregations transform from life-giving centers of spirituality into iron cages of bureaucracies.

We call this phenomenon *the iron cage of congregations*, and it affects more than pastors.[11] Before we began talking to pastors who felt like ministry was no longer working for them, we researched Christian laity who were also struggling with their relationships with the church.[12] They are the dones—those who are done with church but still consider themselves Christians.[13] In other words, they have left the church but have not left the faith.

Along with sociologist Ashleigh Hope, we spoke to over one hundred done Christians, and we learned that one of the major forces pushing the dones out of the church was its bureaucratization. They were frustrated by how the official procedures within their congregations got in the way of serving God. For example, one woman, whom we named "Cora," left the church after she asked if she could start a ministry mowing lawns for the elderly congregants. She says, "There were so many rules and regulations just to mow lawns. . . . I talked to the missions minister, and he told me to come up with a name for my group, propose a budget, write out a mission statement, come to the board hearing, and figure out a way to report back every month. I told him, 'Really?! I just want to mow lawns.'"[14] She left the church for good shortly after this incident. She wanted to love her neighbor, but the church got in the way of this.

The connection between the dones and the pastors we talked to for this study could not be clearer. In fact, the idea for this book arose because of the number of pastors who reached out to us who wanted to be included in the dones study. When churches become overly bureaucratized—when the balance of energy, activity, and attention begins to focus on procedural matters and short-term survival—the best, most talented and dedicated members begin to walk away. That was the astonishing story of the dones. People weren't leaving because they already had one foot out the door. They were highly committed and active members who were leaving because on balance, the church was moving more toward being transactional and losing the elements that make it a transformational space. This is the same story we heard from the pastors in this study.

THE RIGIDITY OF THE IRON CAGE

The iron cage of congregations is more than just bureaucratization in the forms of committees, rules, and regulations. It is also a type of rigidity that constrains pastors from fully living out their calling. It forces pastors to focus on organizational maintenance instead of serving their communities. It hardens congregational life, and life-giving traditions become rigid, getting in the way of spiritual growth. The congregation becomes so inflexible that the organization cannot handle its pastor's nuanced faith.

Charles, the forty-five-year-old former Presbyterian pastor who spoke to us about being authentic in chapter 1, felt the rigidity of congregations while he was serving as the associate pastor in a wealthy, white, suburban church with a large population of retired military veterans. Charles's main frustration was that much of what he did in the church was not what he thought was important in his calling. He was called to serve hurting and marginalized teenagers, and at every turn, his congregation pushed back against that calling.

Charles asked why his church was spending 90 percent of the budget on building maintenance and administration instead of reaching the needy in the community. He was told, "Yeah, but we are doing some good things in here." He questioned why he had a thirty-minute conversation with a committee about the color of the hymnal. He was told, "Yeah, but this is important." Charles called this the "Yeah, but" answer, and he heard it many times over his pastorate.

One of his main frustrations was his congregation's inflexibility with politics and faith. His church was very supportive of the Republican Party, and it often had patriotic elements in its worship services. During the Iraq War of the early 2000s, the senior pastor thanked God for George W. Bush and God leading the president to do the right thing by starting the war. Charles was frustrated by this. He says, "Nothing against patriotism, but my theology states that this is not fitting in a worship environment." Charles brought up his discomfort with the patriotic elements within worship to the leaders of the congregation. They told him, "Yeah, but we've done this for years." As someone who was politically left of center, Charles felt as if he could not fit within the congregation. He concludes, "There was no real line between suburban, White, Republican America and faith. And if that's true, there is something wrong. [*laughs*] I just cannot do it anymore."

Charles ultimately decided to leave congregational ministry because it was so rigid in its set ways that he was unable to fulfill his calling to "hurting people and not to affluent White kids." When we asked why he did not go to another church that focused on marginalized teenagers, he dejectedly stated, "I just didn't see any hope that there will be any real difference. I'm not judging the people. It's just the system. It's the way it's set up. Christians are known for their committees and the paperwork, wasting so much time. I'm not doing this. This is ridiculous." The iron cage of congregations created an environment where Charles could not live up to his calling, and so he left the pastorate. The church was no longer an organization where ministry occurred because it was focused on stability ("We've done this for years") instead of focusing on transformation. Charles is now a probation officer who works with troubled teenagers and finds a deep satisfaction knowing that he is living out his calling to serve. As he closed his interview with us, Charles contentedly stated, "You are better off losing your career than losing your faith and your life."

Lisa also struggled with the fact that the iron cage discourages transformational change and encourages stability. She was, however, surprised by this discovery. Although now working in information technology, she was the pastor of a progressive congregation in the UCC, among the United States' most liberal Christian denominations. Like Charles, she shared that one reason she left the ministry was that the churches she served were not flexible enough to have political conversations with passionate and divergent views. As a Black pastor in a predominately white, progressive congregation, Lisa recognized that there was a learning curve to serving in a different cultural setting. She says, "It was a hard adjustment for me because I was not accustomed to worship in that context, let alone leading worship in that context." Still, after a few months, she adjusted, and as she describes her ministry, "It was lovely and beautiful."

But then Michael Brown, an eighteen-year-old Black teenager, was shot and killed by a white police officer in Ferguson, Missouri, in 2014. That event, and the Black Lives Matter movement that grew out of it, left a powerful impression on Lisa. She and her progressive congregation responded. They spoke about race relations within worship services and held formal dialogues about reconciliation. Lisa says, "It was really a good movement for us as a congregation. We cried together. We shared our experiences, and everything was good."

Everything changed when Lisa hung a Black Lives Matter banner on her congregation's sign. She recounts, "That next week, we got so many phone calls and so much hate mail and angry visits from people in the community—a predominantly white working-class community. They were outraged and angry and just hateful over the sign." She expected some pushback because of "the climate of our nation." However, what shocked her was how her own church responded. Her progressive UCC congregation did not support her and did not take a stand on the issue. She says, "It was me against the community. My congregants stood there with their hands behind their backs like 'This isn't my fight.'" Her congregants worried that she was being too political as a minister. She said that was the moment she realized she would leave congregational ministry. Her ministry and her politics were intertwined. She says, "You cannot separate ministry from social justice. . . . That's not my understanding of the church of Christ." For her, the social justice work within the Black Lives Matter movement was the work the church was called to do. Her congregants felt differently.

Lisa ultimately decided that even though she felt called to lead people spiritually, the congregation was not the avenue in which to pursue her calling. Her congregants were perfectly fine with having political conversations, but similar to Charles's situation with his GOP-leaning church, they were not able to do the transformational work of connecting justice with faith when the community was upset about the congregation's actions. The iron cage, once again, created a rigidity that maintained stability and discouraged change.

Other pastors spoke of how the rigidity of the iron cage was not so much political as it was spiritual. These leaders felt that congregational work actually stifled their spiritual leadership. They wanted to go deeper spiritually, but the structures of their churches kept things shallow. Aaron, a United Methodist pastor in a southern state, strongly believes in the Wesleyan theology that salvation is a lifelong process and is best lived out in small groups of spiritual accountability. He experienced a deep sense of community and spiritual connection with God while a college student, and he believes his calling is to replicate that within local churches. He says, "I know people are hungry for it, but they just lack that experience in their everyday lives with the church."

Aaron recently started a small group within his church to help foster community and his congregants' relationships with God. In a short time, it has been a remarkable success, and he has seen those small group members grow deeper in their faith. He says, "This is what they've always thought was missing and what they've never had in church all their lives. They have never had that level of accountability in being able to share their spiritual lives with one another." And yet the majority of people in Aaron's congregation do not want small groups. He frankly says, "I'm doing this in spite of the institution." The congregation has pushed back because the small group he created was meeting at the same time as the bingo club. The bingo players were frustrated when they lost some of their members to the small group. Aaron says, "I can't put bingo ahead of spiritual formation."

He is frustrated because he sees his congregants having a low view of the church. Instead of it being the group of people who are Christ's hands and feet, many of his church members see it as being one institution among many that helps people develop moral values. Some of his congregants specifically told him they have stopped attending because their children's sports teams teach the same values as the church.

Aaron wants more for his congregation. He wants to push people further and to "hold people accountable for being responsible for their own faith." He wants to challenge people and create a space where they can grow deeper in their relationships with God. But as he pushes for spiritual growth, his congregation pushes back. Instead of doing the difficult work of growing deeper in God, he observes, his congregants want a comfortable place that teaches children a vague sense of values. Consequently, he feels more like a chaplain—one who offers, as he describes, "a caring relationship and walks alongside people in difficult situations." For him, though, challenging people to grow, not offering the comfort of a chaplain, is the calling of a parish pastor. He states the pastor's job is to "equip, to train, to mobilize God's people . . . to reach others for Christ, and to do the work of social justice." He says, "I'm proud to be a pastor who equips people to grow in their faith and reach others." Yet he is frustrated because it is the congregation itself that is stifling spiritual development for his congregants.

CONCLUSION

These pastors felt like their congregations were impeding spiritual development, even though they are the very organizations intended to foster people's relationships with God. Aaron's exasperation is due to his congregation's refusal to grow deeper spiritually, while Lisa's congregation couldn't handle a pastor actively engaged in challenging race relations. Others, like Stephen, Amanda, and Jeff, feel like their congregations operated more like businesses than churches.

The rationalization of congregations creates an organization that is inflexible and geared toward stability. It pushes out those who want to follow God more deeply. People's relationships with God and their growth in that relationship are often not easily quantified, bureaucratized, or made efficient. These more mystical, messier realms of life require flexibility that organizations, such as congregations, have trouble containing.

Other pastors, though, are not struggling with being spiritual leaders while managing the bureaucratic rules, regulations, and schedules of their congregations. Some are simply fighting to keep their organizations alive. In an environment where many churches are declining, the pastors who lead shrinking congregations wrestle with keeping their doors open all the while leading people in their faith. It is to this organizational dynamic of decline that we turn next.

THE TAKEAWAY

- Congregations are both spiritual entities and physical organizations that need resources in order to survive.
- Congregations copy other more successful organizations, often businesses, to compete.
- Some pastors feel that growing their churches' membership and increasing their budgets are the goals of their ministry, but this can interfere with members' spiritual growth.
- Pastors are frustrated when they are expected to manage their churches like they would manage a business.
- Rationalization is the movement toward efficiency and bureaucracy. When congregations rationalize, it can lead to an "iron cage of congregations," which stifles their own and members' spiritual growth.
- Congregations can be so rigid that there is no longer freedom to follow the Spirit's leading.

FOR REFLECTION AND DISCUSSION

For Pastors
- What parts of your job feel like the numbers game?
- How do you find time to make sure your congregation is successful (with enough members or money) but also ensure you have enough time to lead in

more spiritual matters? How does that tension lead to conflict?

- Has your congregation looked to the business community as a model? If so, were the outcomes successful?
- Has your congregation ever been so rigid that it stifled spiritual growth? If so, how?

For Churches, Seminaries, and Denominations

- Do you expect your pastor to be more of a business leader or a spiritual leader? How do you communicate this to him or her?
- Congregational leaders, in what ways is your congregation inflexible and resistant to spiritual growth?
- How can seminaries prepare future ministers to better understand the financial and organizational needs of a congregation in ways that do not restrict spiritual leadership?
- Denominational leaders, do you view your clergy as assets or liabilities? Do your salaries and benefits reflect this?

CHAPTER 4
THE CHANGING RIVERBED

Religions are like rivers: very little of what matters is visible on the surface.
—Andrew Brown and Linda Woodhead, *That Was the Church That Was*

The pastors we interviewed were not only worried that the congregational structure has bureaucratized and squeezed out the Spirit, but they were deeply concerned about the long-term viability of the congregational structure itself. As we stated in the introduction, North America is secularizing, and fewer people think of themselves as part of a religious tradition. Even fewer attend worship services regularly. Churches are experiencing a "concentration effect," where most of the remaining worshippers attend larger churches, leaving smaller churches in a precarious position.[1] Clergy are caught squarely in the middle of this concentration effect because most are not leading these well-resourced, growing large churches. They work in the smaller, and often shrinking, congregations.

This decline in church membership means congregations have fewer resources, so many pastors must work harder just to help their congregations survive.

KEEPING A BUILDING OPEN

Christopher, a forty-six-year-old Lutheran pastor in the Northeast, is deeply frustrated with the crumbling denominational and congregational structures surrounding him. His story begins in another crumbling institution: a family-owned local bank. He worked for the small bank that his family had owned for three generations but saw that its future was untenable. While he looked for other banking jobs in the area, he felt a call to the pastorate. He left his banking career and entered seminary, where he earned an MDiv. After seminary, he received a call to be a pastor at a Lutheran congregation.

As he left one untenable institution, he was unaware that he was entering another whose future was just as uncertain. When going through the call process, the congregation used six-year-old membership rolls and budgets to hide the fact that it was losing members quickly and was not able to pay the full pastor salary recommended by the denomination. After he accepted the call and moved his family, the congregation cut his hours down to half time. He reported his congregation for not meeting salary guidelines to his bishop. His bishop called him into his office, and Christopher reports the bishop saying, "Christopher, I knew we would be having this conversation, but I just didn't think it would be this quickly." The denomination was well aware that his congregation was financially unsound and that it had not been able to pay its pastor's full salary in years. Christopher left the meeting dejected. He says, "Right now, being a pastor is not going to be able to sustain us." In order to survive financially, he began substitute teaching, and his wife took a teaching job 120 miles away. She and the children moved away from the congregation's little town to reduce her commute, leaving Christopher alone most days of the week.

Christopher is desperate. He feels called to be a pastor, but he says, "I feel stuck in a situation that is not what I felt called to do." He wants to find a congregation that could support him as a full-time pastor, where he could serve the community, and where he could see "the work of the Spirit" within his work. Yet the very organizations designed to support his call—the denomination and the congregation—have not allowed him to live out his calling. The denomination was not honest with him when he accepted his position, and the congregation cannot financially support a full-time pastor.

When we asked him if he wanted to leave this specific congregation or if he wanted to leave congregational ministry altogether, he gave a mixed message. He says, "It's still, at this point, the wrong congregation. But there's a growing frustration at the synod and denominational level within me." He is actively seeking other pastoral jobs, but underneath his search is a sense of hesitancy at the sustainability of the institution. He says, "My frustration with potential other calls is a lot of these congregations are smaller [than his current congregation] and just are not fully able to pay a pastor full time." He goes on, "Every little church would love to have a pastor, but every little church can't afford one." At the core of his story is his frustration with an institution designed to support a pastor's calling to preach, serve, and lead, and yet this institution itself was making this impossible.

Helen, sixty, is also struggling to lead a dying organization. For her, this work is a major source of spiritual exhaustion. She is an Episcopal priest, having had a career as a social worker. She previously worked in a nursing home and found herself being a spiritual leader for many of the residents. She felt called to enter into seminary and be ordained as a priest. Now she is the rector of a small church in the Northeast, but she says her pastoral work is draining, especially on Sundays. As an introvert, she acknowledges that being in front of others is *emotionally* exhausting, but for her, the work is *spiritually* exhausting as well. She describes it by saying, "Sundays are just work for me. They are no longer a time of renewal for me anymore. It's the opposite."

At the root of Helen's dissatisfaction is that her church is struggling to stay open. Around forty people attend each week, and the congregation is now spending down its endowment just to pay monthly bills. Instead of focusing on nurturing her parishioners' relationships with God, she now focuses most of her energy on organizational life support. She feels blamed for the struggling congregation. Her evaluation as a priest is based largely on how many people show up each Sunday. Yet she understands that there are larger dynamics outside of her congregation that are affecting the numbers. The town where her congregation resides has a lot of struggling churches, and yet the blame for her church not filling its pews is placed on her. She says, "When things don't go right, it is the clergy's fault. The fact that your church is not full isn't because the community is changing and that there are six big churches on the corners and there aren't enough people to fill them. It's because the priest is not doing his or her job." She continues to feel a profound calling by God to be a spiritual leader, but she says, "I don't think keeping a building open is important."

MAINLINE PROTESTANT DECLINE

Within our sample, the issue of institutional decline was one of the few that were influenced by religious tradition. The pastors who spoke of struggling churches were Mainline Protestants. While pastors in Evangelical congregations worried about the structure of congregations not allowing them to fully live out their calling, very few spoke to us about losing members or being in dire financial circumstances. This is not to say that all Evangelical groups are growing and none are declining. The largest Evangelical denomination, the Southern Baptist Convention (SBC), has experienced a decline in membership since 2006.[2] Still, Evangelical pastors in our sample did not speak about trying to sustain a dying institution. For Evangelicals, the challenge was not about the level of resources but about the level of bureaucracy, a CEO model of ministry, and the spiritual alienation that comes from creating a religious product.

Mainline Protestants, though, were seriously concerned that their institutions were on life support. The data reflect our pastors' personal experiences. Table 4.1 shows the change in membership for the largest Christian denominations in the United States. Every US Mainline Protestant denomination lost members in the first two decades of the twenty-first century. This stands in sharp contrast to the situation of Evangelical Protestant groups and the Roman Catholic Church. Within the Evangelical category, the two Lutheran denominations experienced major declines from 2000 to 2020, as has the Church of the Nazarene.[3] The SBC, the largest Protestant denomination in the United States, has experienced a decline beginning in 2006. From then to 2020, it lost 14 percent of its membership.[4]

The Mainline pastors we spoke to deeply and personally felt the impact of these numbers. They were not just statistics for them, but they were real flesh and blood, brick and mortar. These pastors must reconcile the bills that are due and the budgets that do not quite cover them. They personally know the congregants who leave or die, and they are the ones maintaining the beautiful sanctuaries built to hold many more

Table 4.1: Changes in US denominational membership, 2000–2020

Religious tradition	2000^	2010^	2019/20†	Percent change, 2000–2019/20
Mainline Protestants				
United Methodist Church	8,340,954	7,679,850	6,487,300	–22.2
Evangelical Lutheran Church in America	5,125,919	4,274,855	3,265,581	–36.3
Presbyterian Church (U.S.A.)	3,485,332	2,675,873	1,302,043	–62.6
Episcopal Church	2,333,327	1,951,907	1,798,042	–22.9
American Baptist Churches	1,436,909	1,308,054	1,241,681	–13.6
United Church of Christ	1,377,320	1,058,423	802,356	–41.7
Christian Church (Disciples of Christ)	820,286	639,551	NA	–22.0*
Evangelical Protestants				
Southern Baptist Convention	15,960,308	16,136,044	14,525,579	–9.0
Assemblies of God	2,577,560	3,030,944	3,295,923	27.9

Religious tradition	2000^	2010^	2019/20†	Percent change, 2000–2019/20
Lutheran Church— Missouri Synod	2,554,088	2,278,586	1,861,129	–27.1
Church of God (Cleveland, TN)	895,536	1,074,047	NA	19.9*
Seventh-Day Adventist	880,921	1,060,386	NA	20.4*
Wisconsin Evangelical Lutheran Synod	721,665	385,321	349,014	–51.6
Church of the Nazarene	636,564	649,836	621,278	–2.4
Presbyterian Church in America	306,156	341,482	383,338	25.2
Orthodox Presbyterian Church	26,008	29,842	31,043	19.4
Roman Catholic Church	59,900,000	65,600,000	67,700,000	3.2

^ 2000 and 2010 data are from the Association of Religion Data Archives, www.thearda.com.
† 2019/20 data are self-reported statistics from each tradition's annual report, where available.
* For traditions without 2020 data, the percentage change is from 2000 to 2010.

people in worship. Ultimately, they are in charge of keeping up morale for those who remain behind.

A CHANGING RIVERBED

North American religion is experiencing the effects of secularization, and even some Evangelical Protestant traditions are losing members. But why has the brunt of religious decline chiefly affected Mainline Protestants? This question has concerned sociologists of religion at least since the 1970s, when the pattern first began to show itself, and Dean Kelley of the National Council of Churches wrote *Why Conservative Churches Are Growing* in 1972.[5]

In their analysis of the declining status of the Church of England in English society, journalist Andrew Brown and sociologist Linda Woodhead describe religion as a river.[6] When the river changes from calm waters to white water rapids, it is because the riverbed—and not the water itself—has changed. The very foundations over which the water flows have transitioned from sandy silt to hard rock. This pattern is the same for religions. When a religion experiences a dramatic change, we must look not at the religion itself but at its riverbed, or the society that supports it. Sociologist Mark Chaves suggests four such changes in the foundations of society that have led to the decline in Mainline Protestantism: lower fertility rates, lower rates of youth retention, a weakening connection with the upper social class, and a cultural alignment with the broader society.[7]

One of the major changes in the "riverbed" of North American religion is a change in fertility.[8] Canadians and Americans have fewer children than previous generations because more people live in urban areas, more children survive to adulthood, and more people postpone having children until later in their lives. This massive, society-level change has impacted Mainline Protestants greatly because their birth rates are lower than those of Evangelical Protestants and Catholics.[9] The decline in Mainline churches is not merely an issue of evangelism or recruitment. They are not raising enough future members. With smaller families, fewer children are being born into the faith, and so congregations shrink over time. (Conservative

Protestants are now following this trend, as can be seen with the Southern Baptist decline, but this pattern is in its early stages.[10])

At the same time, Mainline Protestants are not birthing enough new members, and they are also failing to retain the teenagers who were raised in the church. All religious groups experience teenagers leaving the faith, but Mainline youth are more likely to leave and join the ranks of the nones.[11] In the last half of the twentieth century, around one-third of people raised in a Mainline church left the faith, and another 20 percent no longer attended but remained associated with the tradition.[12] This trend is only increasing over time.

Why are Mainline teenagers more likely to leave the fold? Catholic teens also leave the faith, but Catholicism can be a powerful part of one's ethnic identity, especially for those with a Hispanic, Irish, or Italian cultural heritage. This means that Catholic teens are less likely to leave because to do so means to abandon one part of their ethnicities.[13] Mainline Protestantism does not have this connection for its teenagers, as it is not quasi ethnic. Additionally, Mainline Protestants are less likely than Evangelicals to emphasize faith within their family lives.[14] Mainline Protestant congregations dedicate fewer resources to youth groups, youth pastors, and youth events, such as camps.[15] This creates a social environment for Mainline Protestant teenagers that is not as culturally powerful to nurture them in the faith. As a result, Mainline congregations are shrinking faster than congregations in other traditions because their teenagers are leaving at higher rates.

Another change in the riverbed is how North American culture associates social class with religion. Mainline Protestant denominations were historically connected to the upper classes in North America. Episcopalians, Congregationalists, and Presbyterians were more likely to have higher levels of education and incomes and were linked to elite groups and organizations.[16] Conservative Protestants, however, had been considered more on the periphery of society, and their organizations (colleges, publishers, media outlets, and so forth) were not associated with national centers of power. When a North American family moved up in social class, it would often leave its conservative Protestant church and join a Mainline denomination, which grew the Mainline membership rolls. This connection between the well-to-do and Mainline Protestants has now weakened.[17] While Mainline Protestants continue to have higher levels of education and incomes than most other traditions, Evangelical Protestant denominations are no longer considered fringe groups. Well-educated or wealthy Evangelicals now no longer feel the social pressure to join a Mainline Protestant church in order to be viewed as respectable.[18] They can remain Evangelicals and still be connected to the elite, and so this pipeline for Mainline Protestant recruitment has dried up.

In addition to changes in fertility, retention, and social class, the fourth reason Chaves offers for a decline in Mainline Protestants is a cultural alignment with the broader society.[19] Mainline Protestant denominations are more likely to be progressive on issues of women's ordination, LGBTQ inclusion, and racial reconciliation. Evangelical denominations and the Catholic Church, however, often hold the more conservative views—for example, that there are distinct gender roles and that marriage should be between only one man and one woman.[20] While this cultural divergence has been occurring among Mainlines, Evangelicals, and Catholics, North American culture at large has become increasingly more open to women's rights and the acceptance of LGBTQ people into society.[21] In other words, North American culture and Mainline Protestantism are moving in the same direction.

This cultural alignment means two things. First, Mainline Protestants are essentially winning the culture wars.[22] The goals for many Mainline Protestant groups are the same goals as the broader culture: women's full access to leadership, a more robust conversation about racial justice, and equal rights for the LGBTQ community.[23] Second, North Americans who want a community that is supportive of more traditional views of marriage and gender find a refuge in Evangelical churches and conservative Catholic parishes, which bolsters their membership and attendance. On the other hand, when a person looks for a community that advocates for women's rights, LGBTQ inclusion, or deeper conversations about race, she or he can find it in the larger society. They do not necessarily have to join a Mainline congregation because the secular society already advocates for these issues.

Evangelicals and Catholics gain members because there is a distinction, or what sociologists call "tension," between their groups and the larger culture.[24] In a social pattern that may seem counterintuitive, religious traditions that have higher levels of tension with society are actually better able to recruit new members and create a powerful feeling of commitment among the members they already have.[25] By creating a strong sense of "us versus them," conservative traditions increase the devotion their members feel toward their groups, which makes them stronger.[26] So there is a cost to the Mainline Protestant victory in the culture wars. They are no longer as distinct from the culture (they have a lower level of tension) and are therefore less able to create strong communities of faith.

NOSTALGIA AS GRIEF

Glen has personally witnessed firsthand the effects of the changing riverbed in society during his life as a pastor. As a sixty-four-year-old Presbyterian Church (U.S.A.) pastor in the Northeast, he is one year away from retirement. His entire career has been in the ministry, but he is exiting with a dim view of his profession. He believes the entire model of congregational ministry is broken. He named this "the Constantinian model," where the church was the center of the community, Sundays were protected days, children went to Sunday school, and churches had choirs. But he says, "This is not happening anymore."

When he first began in ministry, Glen says he did not know the changes that were about to take place. He says, "I took for granted a whole bunch of things—that there will always be a church as we know it; that there would always be a church hierarchy; that you would need a pastor, associate pastor, organist, choir director, and elders. . . . You just trusted that would always be there." His naivete began to go away the longer he worked within congregations. The things he took for granted were no longer givens in the ministry. He told us he began to realize about a decade ago that "this isn't working, and I'm working harder to do this. I mean really a lot harder. . . . I began to question whether this model could keep going." He could see the model was not working because he was working with fewer resources—both members and money. He says that even the larger Presbyterian churches were reducing staff and losing members. Yet the expectations of ministry did not change. His congregants continued to expect the Constantinian model of ministry: a fully staffed congregation with a wide range of activities for all ages.

At the core of these expectations is a sense of nostalgia, which for Glen is quite painful. He says, "When people talk about the way it used to be, I find that just demeaning and painful to listen to." He angrily thinks out loud to us with a conversation he has replayed in his mind many times. He says, "People say, 'You know, a generation ago, we had a Sunday school full of kids. We had to set up chairs in the sanctuary.' Part of me wants to say, 'Are you telling me that if I worked harder or if I was better, this will happen?! Is that what you're saying?' Because that's not true." He views this nostalgia as ultimately coming from a place of grief in his congregants. He describes his members: "They're grieving for an institution that they once knew and once experienced, and they're in pain."

Glen too is in pain as he prepares for retirement. He has been very successful by many measures of ministry. He has pastored large, high-status congregations. Yet he looks back with some regret, knowing that the model he worked within is no longer sustainable. He says, "I really wonder if I invested in a model that no longer works. Part of it is me being successful at it, yet I wonder if my labors were in vain . . . because I see the institution I have served, and it's just not working anymore."

These weary pastors are on the frontlines of sweeping social changes that are beyond their control. As religious groups continue to lose members, congregational leaders are faced with the sobering reality that their institutions may not be sustainable. Furthermore, these clergy are often held personally accountable for the loss of resources by their denominational managers and their congregants. The end result is that no one is happy. The pastors are unfulfilled because their job is now trying to keep their organizations alive, while the congregants mourn the loss of full pews, children's Sunday schools, and choirs that sing every week. These clergy are working harder with fewer resources, and so they wonder if the congregational model they were called to serve will last.

Yet some expressed hope, for their sense of calling was to serve not an institution but God. In his *Embracing God's Future without Forgetting the Past*, Evangelical Lutheran Church in America pastor Michael Girlinghouse has written a guide for those navigating the grief and nostalgia that come with dying congregations.[27] He guides congregants to express their profound sadness at losing their beloved congregations, but he encourages them ultimately to "remember forward" and to walk boldly into "God's future."[28]

In the midst of his cynicism for local congregational ministry, Glen too was hopeful. He says, "I think my faith is strong and is as informed as ever. But how that faith will be nurtured and supported within some type of institutional setting is a major question for me. Because the institution that I have served—it's just not working anymore. . . . I do think that perhaps God's in the midst of this. . . . I think we're in the midst of this tremendous era of transition, which could be very exciting." He sees the dramatic institutional decline of congregations not as a defeat but as an exciting opportunity. He is not worried that Christianity will cease to exist, but he is hopeful that God is about to do something new. Nevertheless, he is looking forward to retirement, knowing that he can rest from a lifetime of ministry trying to fight institutional decline.

THE TAKEAWAY

- Pastors are leading congregations in the midst of secularization, which means many churches and denominations, often Mainline Protestants, have fewer resources and members.
- Society-wide changes that are outside of pastors' control have led to the decline of Mainline Protestantism.

These changes include lower fertility rates, the decreasing likelihood of retaining teenagers, the decoupling of denominations and higher social classes, and a cultural alignment with the larger society.

- Pastors are held accountable for their congregations' successes and failures, even though these large-scale patterns are driving the changes.
- As a result, pastors feel like they are working harder with fewer resources and seeing diminishing results.

FOR REFLECTION AND DISCUSSION

For Pastors

- Has your congregation experienced a decline over the years? If so, how has this affected your ministry?
- Do you feel like you are working harder with fewer resources? If so, how does that manifest itself?
- What stories does your congregation tell itself about the past? Do you hear stories of the "good old days" in your congregation? Is there a sense of grief and nostalgia among congregants?
- Do you think congregational ministry is sustainable in the future? Why or why not?

For Churches, Seminaries, and Denominations

- In an era of diminishing resources, does your organization operate as if pastors are personally responsible for their congregations' decline or growth?
- Does your organization offer a sustainable model for professional ministry in terms of expectations, benefits, and salaries? In what ways is your model not sustainable?

- How do we faithfully prepare future ministers to lead in an uncertain environment when past successes may not be achievable in the future?
- How do we train our laity and clergy to better understand the social forces affecting congregational ministry?

PART III

STUCK IN THE CAREER

CHAPTER 5
WHY DON'T THEY LEAVE THE MINISTRY?

Let every man abide in the calling wherein he is called and his work will be as sacred as the work of the ministry. It is not what a man does that determines whether his work is sacred or secular, it is why he does it.

—A. W. Tozer, *The Pursuit of God*

Most, if not all, of the pastors we spoke to feel a calling to serve. Some had left the professional ministry in order to find another avenue to fulfill this calling, a topic we will explore in the next chapter. Others continue to serve as pastors while continuing to feel deeply dissatisfied. We wanted to dive deeper into this dynamic, and so we asked the question, "Why stay? Why not find another way to fulfill your calling outside of the congregation?" When we asked this question, we received two general answers. First, some leaders who applied for other positions were stigmatized because they were pastors. Potential employers do not know how to interpret their job experience as religious leaders, and their MDivs from seminary do not translate well to other jobs. Their lack of viable alternatives keeps them within ministry. Second, many pastors feel the pressures of finances. They have school loans to pay or children in college. There is stability within the ministry because the position usually comes with a steady paycheck. So they remain for the money.

THE STIGMA OF THE PROFESSION

Some of our pastors spoke about the nature of the profession itself as a barrier to them leaving the ministry in order to pursue other opportunities. Potential employers often do not realize that the work of clergy is very diverse. They raise money; manage budgets; identify, recruit, and retain talent; develop programs and events; cultivate stakeholders; and oversee property and volunteers, often at sizeable levels.[1] These skills are in high demand in many careers. But these are not the experiences and skills that come to mind when potential employers see a pastoral position on a résumé. For their part, clergy also often seem not to understand how to translate their experience onto a résumé in a way that catches the eye of potential employers.

Jeff, the recently resigned American Baptist pastor, describes the pastorate as one of the last generalist occupations there is. He says, "Well, as a minister, you're not just someone who preaches, but you're also a chief executive. Depending on the size of your church, you have to be the chief cook and bottle washer as well. You have to be not just proficient but pretty good at a whole bunch of different skills and abilities." Potential employers may not understand the skill set that clergy have and therefore may not hire people with a pastoral background.[2] Jeff is frustrated by this dynamic. He is looking for a job outside of congregational ministry. After sending out many job applications and résumés, he's had little success. He believes the word *pastor* on a résumé kills his job prospects. He says, "Getting interviews is very difficult because when you see 'pastor' on the résumé, it essentially discounts the file. . . . It's difficult to get people to listen to you, to even explain yourself when they don't understand what the clergy job even is." He goes on to ask, "What other job carries a stigma so bad that employers just take the résumé out?"

Jeff's insight into the idea of "stigma" is telling. It may not only be that potential employers simply misunderstand the nature of clergy work. Instead, employers may have a negative bias against clergy, which makes them less likely to hire pastors. Jeff's intuition about the stigma clergy carry is increasingly being shown by the data. Over the past decades, the status of the clergy profession has declined. Each year, Gallup asks Americans how trustworthy they think different professions are. Nurses are always at the top of the list, but Americans' views of the clergy have drifted significantly downward since the first poll in 1976.[3] In 1978, 61 percent of Americans viewed the clergy as being honest and ethical. Now in the wake of clergy sex abuse scandals, this decreased to 40 percent by 2020. Furthermore, Americans seek out clergy for advice less often,[4] and fewer top college graduates want to go into the ministry.[5] Consequently, the profession of clergy may be viewed so negatively that those who have the word *pastor* on their résumés may be less likely to be hired. Brian, a forty-five-year-old ex-Evangelical pastor in the Midwest, even considered taking his twelve years of pastoral work off his résumé entirely. He tells us, "But because of my job experience, they [the potential employers] look at ministry as if I told them, 'Well, you know, I've spent the last twelve years over at Hogwarts!'" Brian goes on to explain, "Once you've been out of the traditional job market for a decade, those skills are null and void. They don't matter anymore."

Similarly, Adam, the former nondenominational youth pastor, had experience with the stigma of the clergy profession. As he tried to transition from his youth pastoring job, he evaluated his skill set as a youth pastor. He decided that working for the government or a department of recreation would align nicely with his skills in event planning, budget management, and volunteer recruitment. Yet he encountered roadblocks with each job application. When he was finally rejected as the youth coordinator for a city's recreation center, he asked the hiring manager if she could provide any tips on how to make his future applications better. Adam reports that she responded, "Your experience at the church really doesn't do anything for us." He sounds dejected when he tells us, "They looked at my experience and the church like it was nothing."

This potential employer's response is important. It signals that she did not count Adam's clergy work as valid. The stigma associated with the clergy profession negated his entire career as a pastor. His work managing a large youth organization (over one hundred teenagers), balancing budgets, and planning major events was discounted so much that the hiring manager treated him as having no job experience whatsoever. He is now finishing a graduate degree in recreation so he can have the appropriate credential needed to work for a parks and recreation department.

While some pastors were viewed as *under*qualified, others told us that they were not hired because employers viewed them as *over*qualified, especially if they had the MDiv, the standard credential from a seminary. This graduate degree makes them overqualified for many entry-level positions. Furthermore, the degree is solely focused on ministry, and so employers view the degree with a certain level of suspicion or even ignorance. The pastors in this study were frustrated because they were highly educated professionals, but their education did not transfer into the world beyond the church.

Kenneth is a fifty-year-old pastor in the Northeast within the Evangelical Lutheran Church in America (ELCA). He left his last pastorate of ten years because his small congregation was not able to pay a pastor full time. To help with his bills, he applied for jobs at the post office, a grocery store, and a large distribution center for Walmart. As he was walking out of the interview with Walmart, he received a rejection email. He asked around his community why he, as an educated professional, could not get a minimum wage job in his community. Over and over, he heard the same message: "They won't hire anyone with a master's degree."

Part of Kenneth's frustration in his job search is his discontent with the MDiv. He laments to us, "An MDiv is the most useless, worthless degree you can possibly have because it doesn't do anything for you. There is nothing useful about it. It is completely only for an occupation in a church."

It is true that this degree was designed to prepare clergy for ordained ministry within congregations, and most Mainline Protestant denominations, like the ELCA, require it for ordination. As a professional program meant to train pastors, it is one of the longest master's degree programs in North America, requiring a minimum of three years of graduate work in Scripture, history, theology, and pastoral leadership.

Yet this massive educational investment may actually hinder seminary graduates if they decide to transition out of the ministry. Like Adam and Jeff, Kenneth viewed the MDiv itself as having a certain stigma associated with it—guilt by association. In an environment where national conversations about clergy often revolve around abuse, scandal, and corruption, being associated with the pastoral role may lead potential employers to assume that *any* clergy is guilty of these characteristics. Kenneth describes what he imagines is the response from those looking at his application: "If you fill out your résumé and you've got an MDiv, the church has such a negative reputation now across the country that I bet an employer looks at that and says, 'Oh my God! He's one of those pastors! We're not going to hire one of those bastards!'"

The stigma against clergy need not even be overt to still carry very real ramifications. Although there are legal protections in place allowing employees at most companies to engage in voluntary religious conversations with one another, the increasing focus on and need to maintain an atmosphere that is free from discrimination—inclusive and welcoming to all—might keep some employers from looking at former clergy for open positions. The Anti-Defamation League notes, "EEOC [Equal Employment Opportunity Commission] religion-based charges of discrimination have increased approximately 52% since 1997," which might contribute to a human resource professional's reluctance to hire former pastors, even if they do not harbor such overt feelings as Kenneth describes above.[6]

Stigmas are powerful within social life. As the sociologist Erving Goffman describes, a stigma is any characteristic that can be socially "discrediting."[7] The stigmatization of the clergy is a symptom of larger social processes, and these pastors are unfortunately caught in the middle. First, as we have outlined in this book, fewer people are religious, and therefore clergy are not leaders within these people's social spheres. Second, even fewer people are active members of religious congregations, and so they rarely come into contact with clergy. These lower membership rates are compounded by the trend that greater numbers of Americans distrust clergy because of the clergy sexual abuse scandals. All of these trends mean that the profession of clergy has a stigma problem. The characteristics traditionally associated with the clergy—a graduate-level education from a seminary and generalist skills leading an organization—are now being viewed negatively by the larger public, and the result is these pastors who want to leave the profession are unable to make the transition.

FINANCIAL STABILITY

Not every pastor who wanted out felt like the clergy profession was stigmatized. Others were hesitant to leave because their career as a minister offered financial stability. While pastors do not make exorbitant amounts of money when compared to other professions with graduate degrees, they do make a middle-class income when their congregations can afford a full-time salary. In the United States, the Bureau of Labor Statistics estimates that clergy within congregational ministry made an average salary of $54,000 for the year 2020.[8] This means most Protestant ministers are neither in poverty nor wealthy. This steady income is a major deterrent for those dissatisfied pastors who would otherwise consider leaving the profession.

Glen, the soon-to-be-retiring Presbyterian pastor from chapter 4, keenly understands the financial stability that being a pastor brings. At age sixty-four, he looks back over his forty years in ministry and sees a change. When he first began serving congregations, churches were flourishing. Sunday schools had children in them, the choirs were led by full-time directors, and the pews were full. He became very successful in his ministry. He pastored large congregations and was even a denominational leader within the Presbyterian Church (U.S.A.). Yet Glen notes, around eighteen years ago, this model began to erode, and churches began to fail: "I was able to keep going and fairly function at a high level, but even as I was functioning at that level, it was harder and harder. . . . Something is going on in the culture. Something is happening in the church."

Glen was having more difficulty maintaining a high level of success, and so he thought about getting out of ministry. He knew this would take a financial toll on him and his family. Glen says, "I was invested in a pension plan; I've got a child in college and soon to be going to graduate school. There were a lot of family considerations that helped me keep in this." He decided to stay and work as a Presbyterian pastor until he retired. He describes this decision as "a lack of courage." He goes on: "Let's call it what it is—perhaps a lack of courage, a lack of self-examination—and really sitting down and examining what was going on and just your simple concern for the welfare of my family. I mean, I could make, and I did make, and I am making a good living, a very comfortable living right now." Because of his decision to stay in the ministry, his family is financially stable, he does not have a mortgage, and his retirement is secure. Yet he looks back on his choice with some sadness. Glen says, "I know there's something wrong. I know there's something more going on. Maybe what I'm dealing with is some guilt—who knows? It is guilt, let's name it. If I had more courage, it could have been different." Glen chose to prioritize his family's financial welfare and remain in ministry. He stayed within a system of failing churches and shrinking budgets in order to continue to provide for his family and secure his future retirement. Many would view his choice positively—as a sign of self-sacrifice and patient long-suffering, and yet Glen negatively interprets this as a lack of courage. Regardless of how one interprets the morality of Glen's decision to stay, one thing is clear: it wasn't about a calling.

The national survey data around financial stability back up Glen's experience. Finances are important to ministers. In a 2009 national survey of American clergy, 76 percent said financial well-being was either of "great importance" or "somewhat important" to sustaining their commitment to pastoral ministry (table 5.1). When we break down these survey data even further, we see that there is a relationship between thinking about leaving ministry for a secular job and believing that financial well-being is important in sustaining ministry. Table 5.2 shows that for clergy who think finances are of "little importance" to sustaining their pastoral ministry, just 8 percent have thought about leaving for a secular job within the past year. Yet for those who think of finances as of "great importance" for keeping them in ministry, 43 percent

Table 5.1: Pastors who say financial well-being is important in sustaining their commitment to pastoral ministry

	2001	2009
Great importance	25%	15%
Somewhat important	53%	61%
Somewhat unimportant	11%	20%
Little importance	11%	3%
N	*881*	*681*

Sources: Pulpit and Pew National Survey of Pastoral Leaders (2001) and US Congregational Life Survey (2008/9).
Data are weighted to account for congregational size.

Table 5.2: The importance of financial well-being in sustaining a commitment to ministry by the question, Has the pastor ever thought of leaving ministry for a secular job?

Financial well-being	Never thought of leaving	Thought of leaving
Great importance	57%	43%
Somewhat important	62%	38%
Somewhat unimportant	84%	16%
Little importance	92%	8%
N	*673*	

Source: US Congregational Life Survey (2008/9).
Chi-square (3) = 17.75, p < 0.001.
Data are weighted to account for congregational size.

have thought about leaving for a secular job at least one time in the past year. In other words, the greater emphasis a clergyperson puts on financial well-being, the more likely he or she will think about leaving the ministry for a secular job.

Nancy, the sixty-seven-year-old Episcopal priest who struggles with authenticity and managing a dying congregation (chapters 1 and 3), is remaining within the ministry because of finances. Before she went to seminary and was ordained a priest, she was a nurse and worked in clinics and hospitals. Yet she left this steady job at the age of forty-eight because she felt a strong calling into the ordained ministry. She describes her calling in mystical, powerful language. She says, "It's really hard to get words around it, but in a way, it's a sense of being involved with people across the stages of their lives and offering . . . a sense of the spiritual, a sense of being in touch with—I can hardly come up with the right word—with the Divine, with the Holy." Even with this powerful calling, she focuses on finances when explaining that she remains in the pastorate because, as she says, "I'd like to retire someday." Unlike pastors who did not have a career before they began their ministry, she has a background in nursing, a profession to which she could reasonably return. Yet she says, "I didn't want to go back into nursing—the other thing I could have done—but staying with this for another few years seemed better." We asked her how staying in the ministry was better, and she replied, "In terms of income." She is a single mother who put her daughter through college, which left her with some educational debt. She says, "Realistically and practically speaking, to make a level of income that will keep me going and help me pay down my debt, I'm better off staying with what I do, although I suppose in some ways it would be nice to not have to." She has multiple "push" and "pull" factors keeping her within the ministry.[9] She has a strong sense of divine calling to help people connect with the Holy, but she also struggles with being authentic with her parishioners and is tired of trying to keep a dying congregation alive. Yet when she speaks about what is keeping her in the ministry, she mentions not her calling but her debt.

Aaron too says finances are the number one reason he stays within ministry. As he recounts in chapter 3, he is frustrated by the lack of spiritual activity within his United Methodist congregation. When we ask him why he has not quit the pastorate, he replies, "I actually have two reasons. The primary one, sadly, is financial. I know that's horrible for someone in my position." He goes on to describe how his seminary debt plus the cost of day care for his daughter are prohibitive to his leaving the ministry. He says, "We just cannot *not* be in full-time positions." He then offers a second reason for staying in his calling: "I don't know where else to find that outlet to do the work that I feel called to do."

Aaron has mixed feelings toward his focus on finances. He regrets that money is the driving force within his ministry, but his salary does offer his family some amount of security. He says, "I know ministry is not primarily about the job. It's not about the money. . . . We are mainly on salary, and it's $40,000, which isn't so bad. It's more than I've made in my life. . . . I don't care about the money other than for the security of my family." This ambivalence stems from his belief that ministry should not be focused on the practical, material aspects of life ("It's not about the money"), but he must contend with the fact that there are real-world implications to having a family and paying down school debt.

The tension between the spiritual side of ministry and the practical aspects of supporting oneself is not a recent development. Even the New Testament addresses this issue. In 1 Corinthians 9, Paul tells the readers that those who preach and teach should be able to earn a living from this work. He quotes Deuteronomy 25:4: "You shall not muzzle an ox while it is treading out the grain" (1 Cor 9:9). He then chides the Corinthians: "If we have sown spiritual good among you, is it too much if we reap your material benefits?" (1 Cor 9:11). These pastors, however, are confronting a different reality within this tension between ministry and money. Being a leader in the church of the first century, when the New Testament was written, was a very insecure situation, and so Paul had to advocate for early leaders' wages. A clergyperson in the twenty-first century is in a profession that offers salaries, health insurance, and pensions. Leaving the ministry often requires these pastors to give up a secure financial situation for few other well-paying options.

As professionals, these pastors' experiences reinforce research that describes the middle class as being in a tenuous situation.[10] Well educated but burdened with school loans and childcare costs, many middle-class families make a large enough salary to be comfortable, but they are one paycheck away from financial ruin. As journalist Alissa Quart describes their situation, the middle class is "squeezed" in America because they are hypereducated and yet poor.[11] Many clergy in our study feel this squeeze. Even though their pastoral positions are not lucrative, they are secure and offer a way to pay down their debt or have their children in day care. These pastors stay in the church because there is a paycheck. For other pastors in our study, however, the money was not enough to keep them within the ministry.

Next, we turn to those who have officially left. While they are no longer pastors, many are still trying to fulfill their calling in other creative ways.

THE TAKEAWAY

- Some pastors want to leave the ministry but experience barriers to moving out of the profession.
- One such barrier is the stigmatization of the clergy role. Prospective employers do not fully appreciate the work experience of pastors, or they discredit the profession altogether.
- The MDiv as a degree is misunderstood and does not help clergy find employment outside of the ministry.
- Other clergy stay in the profession because of the steady middle-class income and benefits it provides.

FOR REFLECTION AND DISCUSSION

For Pastors
- What is being in one of the last "generalist" occupations like? How well do people outside the ministry understand what you actually do in your job?

- Do you ever feel stigmatized for being a pastor? How do others' views of your work affect your relationships with friends, family members, or even strangers in your community?
- Do you think your professional skills in leading an organization, writing, public speaking, and textual interpretation are translatable to other fields? If so, how would you clearly communicate their value to a person outside the ministry?
- How do your salary and benefits affect how you think about your job? Do they keep you from moving on to other opportunities?

For Churches, Seminaries, and Denominations
- How can we improve the image of the clergy in the larger community? Why has it taken such a hit?
- What are the benefits of requiring clergy to have the MDiv? What are the drawbacks?

CHAPTER 6
LEAVING THE MINISTRY TO FOLLOW THE CALL

> Most pastors don't leave the ministry because they're rejecting God; they leave the ministry so they can find God again.
> —A. J. Swoboda, *The Dusty Ones*

Peter knew he had to leave congregational ministry. As described in chapter 1, he hated what he felt was the "pretense" within his church that kept people from being fully authentic. He passionately tells us, "I think pretense is a banner over a lot of institutional churches right now. It's a huge, gigantic, all-capitals banner—PRETENSE—and it discourages authenticity and dialogue and relationship."

For him, as a pastor in a large Evangelical church, leaving was not an easy thing to do. He and his wife talked about what their life would look like if he left full-time congregational ministry. They looked at the transition out of the congregation as an adventure and used the Bible for inspiration. He says, "It was adventurous. It was so spontaneous, and it almost looked like the book of Acts and seeing Paul going from town to town." He then interprets his change through the biblical pattern of a death and resurrection. He says, "We're walking out of here, and we don't know if we are going to make it or not. We told each other we're going to die trying. If we're going to be transformed, we're going to die to ourselves. We're going to really die, and death is a painful thing. . . . So let's take the risk."

The risk Peter and his wife took was to create a nonprofit coffee shop, or as he describes it, his "coffee ministry." He loves his new ministry because it lacks the sense of pretense that he felt in the institutional church. He says, "When we got into the coffee ministry, it changed me a lot because people came in and they were broken, and they were real. And I had no idea if a person had accepted Jesus Christ as their Lord and Savior or not. There were times when people would share their hurts with me and I would say, 'Can I say a quick prayer for you?' And they always said yes. They always said yes. I had no idea if they were Jewish, Muslim, or whatever. I just assumed that they had some type of spiritual connection." For over four years, Peter's coffee ministry allowed him to be authentic and to connect with others on a spiritual level. Yet it was financially unstable, and he and his wife had to shut the coffee shop down.

He then got, as he calls it, "a real job" managing two storage facilities. To make this transition, he and his wife took out a home equity loan, but he believes the debt is worth it. He loves his new job at the storage units because it allows him to be fully authentic with the people he works with. He has spiritual conversations at his work, but now he does not have to filter out what he says in fear of losing his job. He says, "And it always surprises me, and humbles me, because I'm able to share what I really, really think and believe. I can actually give my opinion. . . . I can take that risk." In an ironic twist, it was risky for him to be honest and vulnerable about faith when he was a pastor, a career that is centrally about faith. Yet now he feels the freedom to be fully authentic while he is the manager of these storage units, a decidedly "secular" job.

We asked him if this career change has improved his spiritual life. He immediately says, "Absolutely!" He attends a gathering that could be described as a house church. About twenty people gather for a free and open discussion on the Bible. They do not focus on theological controversies, like the inerrancy of Scriptures (the idea the Bible is free from errors), but instead, they focus on Christ and his call "to die to ourselves and allow others to be served." He says, "The freedom to be able to grow with that [honest discussion] and to focus strictly on Christ is so deep and so intimate." He experienced a positive change by leaving the pastorate. His work as a minister hindered him from being honest, open, and vulnerable about spirituality. Even though he works in a very mundane job at the storage facility, he has experienced a spiritual transformation that has led him to feel closer to God.

There have been alarmist claims that pastors are leaving the ministry in record numbers. Some news articles falsely claim that 85 percent of seminary graduates entering the ministry leave within five years and that "90% of all pastors will not stay to retirement."[1] The data do not back up these bold claims. I (Ferguson) have researched seminary graduates and their career aspirations.[2] Only 17 percent of MDiv graduates do not see themselves in the ministry five years after graduating from seminary. This research, though, is prospective and asks how seminarians view their future careers. It is even more difficult to measure exactly how many pastors leave the ministry each year. Most denominations or congregations do not conduct exit interviews, and so the best estimate is that around 1 to 2 percent of both Protestant and Catholic clergy leave the profession each year.[3] That means that this is rare but not unheard of.

Sociologists Dean Hoge and Jacqueline Wenger wrote the seminal book on clergy who leave congregational ministry, *Pastors in Transition*.[4] They interviewed or surveyed over nine hundred former Protestant congregational pastors to ask why they left. Many left to continue in some other type of ministry, while others left because of conflict within their churches. But Hoge and Wenger's major discovery in this book was that pastors overwhelmingly did not leave because of personal problems, like a loss of faith or financial difficulties. They left because organizational and relational pressures pushed them out.[5] These pastors felt unsupported by their churches and denominations or struggled to balance their ministry lives with their family lives.

Not every "stuck" pastor we spoke to remained in the ministry, hemmed in by finances or by the inability to get another job, however. Some realize they must get out, and only when they leave do they recognize they are now better able to fulfill God's calling in their lives. Ultimately, we discover from stuck pastors that at the heart of these decisions to leave the profession is a desire to connect more deeply with others and build stronger, more authentic communities. For clergy who feel stuck, the congregation is no longer the place for connection or community, and they had to find it elsewhere. In many ways, this mirrors the broad findings from my (Packard) previous book *Church Refugees*, which focuses not on pastors but on church members leaving organized religion. They too pointed out that they were leaving the institutional church in order to be more engaged with their faith and their local communities.

GETTING IN THE WAY OF THE CALLING

Charles, a former Presbyterian (U.S.A.) pastor, left congregational ministry when he was in a dark place. As described in chapters 1 and 2, he thought he could not be fully authentic with his congregation, and so he began drinking, gaining weight, and watching his marriage dissolve. He was angry because he saw that a person's relationship with God had no impact on how people in his congregation lived their lives. He says, "I wanted to make a difference. If faith is real, I wanted to go [say], 'OK, this should mean something.' And I found that most people were just living this 'I go to church, and I do whatever the hell I want the rest of the week.'" He tried to get his congregation to refocus on theological matters, but he felt rebuffed by his church every time he brought up something challenging. He tells us that church members would often respond, "Oh, no. Don't bring that up. That might ruffle some feathers." The core issue with his dissatisfaction was that he did not want to risk upsetting the people in his congregation because they were the ones who could fire him. He reinforces the paycheck-authenticity issue discussed in chapter 2 by saying, "I think the biggest issue is the way it's set up now—where your paycheck is directly tied to congregants who give money based on your performance. There's something really wrong with that because you can't call someone out when they are the ones paying the check. And that's why most churches won't do anything prophetic."

He became bitterer as he watched the church focus on institutional maintenance and right-wing politics, while he thought they should be reaching out to hurting people. He tells us, "So much of what you do as a pastor is not what you think is important. And that for me, especially, it just drove me crazy." He was tired of the myriad of meetings and using

90 percent of the church budget on administration instead of helping people. He interprets his distaste through the lens of Scripture. He says, "There is a story in the Bible—the rich, young ruler who went away sad because he has many things. Most of it, your job as a pastor—this is in suburban, upper-middle-class America—they want you to kiss their ass and make them feel good. I couldn't do it anymore." He is clear that his leaving congregational ministry was not about losing his faith. It was about his frustration serving a congregation that he thought focused on the wrong things. He thought about switching churches and getting another job as a pastor. He says, "I easily could have found some church that said, 'We have a nice young pastor, a good-looking wife' and all this stuff. And I easily could have gone to that place and had it made. I could have made more money, but I think I realized that it was all just bullshit. It was never a faith issue. It was 'Jesus love me but save me from your followers!'"

He left the ministry so he could follow his calling. He entered seminary because he wanted to help those who were hurting and needy, and after ordination, he realized that the church was not the venue to do this. To help him make the transition out of congregational ministry, he attended a three-day intensive workshop focused on vocational counseling. He took personality and aptitude tests while receiving individual psychotherapy. As he revealed that he was thinking about leaving the ministry, the workshop leaders gave him very practical advice. First, they recommended he leave the ministry now as a thirty-four-year-old because at forty-five years old, he was going to have a much tougher time finding a job outside the church. Second, they told him to expect to start at the bottom of his new career. He recalls the leaders telling him that no employer is going to think, "Oh, you were a pastor. We are going to make you CEO of our company."

He took this advice, knowing that he was going to have to work his way up in a new career. He used his social networks and his bachelor's degree in psychology to get a counselor position at a youth residential treatment center. The work was challenging, and he took a major pay cut, but he loved it. As he worked as a counselor within the treatment facility, he saw that the probation officers were the ones that actually had a lasting effect on the kids' lives. He did not know much about probation work and began asking around. He realized that probation work is different from being a police officer or being a parole officer. Instead, it is "very much like social work." He began volunteering as a probation officer, and they finally offered him a part-time job. This transitioned to a full-time career, which he has been in for eight years now.

Charles's story reflects one of the central themes of this book: *clergy leave the ministry because in their experiences, their congregations get in the way of their calling.* Charles strongly feels a calling from God to serve those who are hurting. He loves being a probation officer because he gets to work with hurting teenagers and move society toward justice. He says, "We're trying to keep people out of prison, so it's much more restorative, justice oriented—much more treatment oriented." He knows he made the right decision to leave the ministry. He says, "I'm very thankful I got out when I did because I've got a great career, and I can pay all my bills, pay for my kid's college in forty hours a week, which is awesome."

THE CHURCH IS ABSENT IN THE DEAD OF NIGHT

Peter's and Charles's transitions out of the ministry were both successful. They both found meaningful work that allowed them to express their calling. Other former pastors are not so lucky. Some struggle to adjust to a new life outside of congregational ministry. Brian, a forty-five-year-old former Evangelical pastor from the Midwest, is one who is foundering. While leading his previous congregation, he discovered the tension between his calling to be a spiritual leader and the day-to-day work that pastors must do to make their congregations function as organizations. Pastors must plan services, maintain buildings, balance budgets, and recruit the type of members who will support their congregations with their time and money. These organizational goals are often at odds with serving the less fortunate or helping people develop a deeper spirituality. Brian, unfortunately, experienced this tension between reaching out to hurting people and maintaining an organization, and he has yet to find a happy resolution.

He was the pastor of a small church that had a very active youth outreach program. He was a progressive pastor within an Evangelical tradition, and his "heart and soul" was working with the youth group. This group attracted teenagers who had been rejected by society: LGBT teens, "cutters" (those who inflict self-harm), and kids who had experienced sexual or physical abuse. He loved being able to offer these teenagers a safe space to experience God. Yet as he focused more on youth outreach, he often ignored his role of managing the organization to make sure it survived. His congregation was small with few resources, so when his attention turned solely to the teenagers, his church fell apart. He says, "We lost the financial sustainability that we needed to keep the office space, the building, and to be able to fund what we were doing." He needed money because he was financially responsible for the congregation, and so he took a night shift as a taxi driver in his city's downtown area in order to pay the church's bills.

He worked the graveyard shift as a taxi driver for six months before he realized that he was not going back into full-time ministry. He always thought that being a pastor was a lifelong vocation. He was sure he would retire from his congregation one day. Yet as he drove around at night, he learned things about people that he had not realized while serving as a minister and living in his "Christian bubble." He says, "When you're a minister trying to reach down to people like the rest, you understand them differently than when the prostitute, or the homeless person, or the junkie is in your back seat." He realized that the church often ignored these people riding in his back seat during the middle of the night, and he wondered about the church's impact on a community. He says, "The longer that I spent in the taxi, the more impotent I felt the church was in modern society."

One moment particularly struck him and demonstrated the church's "impotence." On a cold night, with temperatures well below freezing, a homeless woman died from exposure at a bus stop. He knew this woman from driving his taxi. He says, "She died within a mile's walk from three different homeless shelters. They could have taken her in, but they wouldn't because she had mental health issues and was a very difficult person to deal with. But they were, in my opinion—and by default we were—complicit in her death. So I felt this loss, and this loss also changed a lot in me." He was moved by this experience because he did not see the church doing anything to save this woman. The church was not a presence in the dark hours when he was driving around drunken partiers, drug users, johns, and the homeless. He bleakly describes it as, "The church was completely absent in the dead of the night."

During the long hours of the night, while he was waiting for a fare, he began to read books on philosophy, comparative religions, and science. His faith began to change, and soon he began to question God's existence. Out of all the pastors in our study, only Brian considers himself an agnostic. He sometimes prays, and other times, he does not think there is a

God who is listening. He describes his current understanding: "I sort of followed in the footsteps of Neil deGrasse Tyson [a famous astrophysicist] in that I'd say I don't know what's out there. I don't really care. It doesn't pertain to my life. I can be an atheist, but sometimes when I'm having really deep emotional moments, I still pray, and I have to lean into that tension." He is no longer a taxi driver, but he is struggling to find a job that suits him. Like the other pastors described in chapter 5, he has had a difficult time translating his résumé to fit nonministerial positions. Employers do not know what to do with his bachelor's degree in "pastoral studies" from a Bible college or with his experience as a pastor.

Yet he also has an "impulse" to serve people. He describes it: "I no longer ever want to go back as an employee of institutionalized religion. But that impulse to still help people, that impulse to move people, that impulse to do something is a part of me and always will be." He has yet to find the right position. Sometimes he gets work as a freelance photographer, and seeing people emotionally connect to his artwork in galleries brings him a lot of joy. He has bounced around between other full-time jobs but is currently in a position selling technology services, though he is miserable. He says, "I hate sales with a passion. I'm good at it, but I hate it!" He is dissatisfied with his life in its present situation. He says, "I'm currently stuck in this space right now."

CONNECTION AND COMMUNITY

When we spoke to former pastors about their experiences leaving full-time ministry, their stories and paths were quite varied. Some, like Charles and Peter, experienced positive changes and newfound senses of freedom. Others, like Brian, were still struggling to find a place in their new realities after leaving the professional ministry. Yet one theme we often heard was that these former ministers continued to search for community and connection. Even if they were not serving in congregations in the formal role as pastors (and even if they no longer participated in congregations), most wanted to live in ways that were more connected to others and more deeply embedded in community than what they experienced in their previous pastoral careers.

The role of a pastor has a significant impact on a person's identity. It shapes how he or she thinks about themselves, and the role often originates from a sense of divine calling. It leaves an indelible mark on a person. Sociologists would describe being a pastor as a "master status," or an identity that affects every other identity a person inhabits.[6] People understand their other roles through their master statuses. Pastors interpret how they interact with their neighborhoods or how they see themselves as parents or spouses through their status as pastors.

One of the key functions of the pastoral role is to create a sense of community and connectedness. When these former clergy leave the profession, the longing for community and connection that was inherent in the pastoral role does not stop. As a former master status, it continues to be a part of their identities, and it shapes how they interpret their next careers. Peter interprets his new career as a storage unit manager using the framework of connecting authentically with others and not having to filter his thoughts. Charles sees his position as a probation officer as one that enables him to bring justice to the community and improve the lives of others. Even Brian, who is struggling to find a career he loves, relishes connecting with people through his freelance photography work.

This theme of connection and community can be most clearly seen in Robert, a forty-four-year-old former pastor in the West. As the worship leader for a large Evangelical congregation, he was pushing fourteen- to fifteen-hour days setting up for the multiple services his church held each Saturday and Sunday. His wife was working full time in the medical field, and they were raising two children. He was running on fumes. When his senior pastor asked why he was not working *more* hours, he knew his church was a toxic place. He left the ministry for a year and a half while he "recovered" and was a stay-at-home dad.

One day, Robert's friend asked him to meet him downtown to see a vacant building that had just become available for rent next to the restaurant he owned. When they walked in, they were horrified. Robert describes it: "It was nasty! I cannot tell you how disgusting it was. Years and years ago, this had been a music store, . . . [but now] it was a brothel. It was a full-blown meth-house brothel that existed right in the middle of downtown." Yet even among the boarded-up windows, repulsive smell, and floor-to-ceiling stripper pole, he immediately knew what this place would become. He told his friend, "This should be a teahouse."

The reason he knew this would be a teahouse was that five years before he saw the abandoned brothel, his wife had a spiritual vision while they were in a worship service. She clearly perceived from God that she and her husband would one day have a business that financed anti–sex trafficking ministries. He recalls his wife saying, "Robert, I don't know how this is going to work out, but this is something we have to do. We are supposed to have some business that will fund this kind of work, and it's going to happen in the next five years." He was standing in the middle of the former brothel with his wife's vision in his mind, knowing that this was the place to create a business. While he and his wife were financially stable because of her job, he was reluctant to take a big risk. But things fell into place. A wealthy friend offered him 50 percent of the teahouse's funding as a silent partner, and so he had enough capital to start his new business.

We interviewed him in his teahouse. It was a lively scene. Music was playing, and customers came in and out to buy tea, coffee, or beer. Proceeds from the shop fund work that gets women out of sex trafficking. He says, "This is in some small way our contribution to fulfilling part of that grand vision that my wife had." While he is no longer serving on a congregation's staff, he feels called by God to do this work. He says, "I look around and ask, 'How did this happen?' Like, honest to God, how did this happen? How did I get here? . . . And so even on the days that I doubt this place, that I doubt myself, I know that we are supposed to be here."

Robert is no longer a pastor, but his identity continues to be shaped by the desire to create a strong community where people connect with one another. He says, "My heart has always been to help build community, and that is something that we do here. People consider this a safe place for them to come. Families come here." He goes on to describe how he has woven his teahouse into the "fabric" of his city's downtown by connecting with other businesses. His shop sells the local bakery's pastries and the neighborhood brewery's beer, so each local business is tied with another. He specifically interprets this desire to build a robust community as a calling: "I do think we are supposed to be here because of the impact we have with other businesses. We know we are supposed to be here in terms of that call that my wife and I personally have. And I know we are supposed to be here for the community that has developed here from people who just didn't have a home." While he does not get paid by a church, his work at the teahouse echoes themes of pastoral ministry. He works for justice by supporting anti–sex work ministries.

He builds community by offering a third space where families can gather, and he reaches out to those who "didn't have a home."

Master statuses are notoriously difficult to leave.[7] They change a person forever because her or his identity has been wrapped up in the master status. The pastoral role creates an indelible mark on those who leave the ministry because the identity is so powerful. For this reason, leaving the pastorate is complicated and not often straightforward.[8] Clergy do not enter another career without being changed by their experiences leading congregations. Often, these former pastors continue to feel a strong sense of calling to serve, to lead others spiritually, and to create deep connections, even if they do not know how to find this outside of congregations.

For instance, Lisa, the United Church of Christ pastor who left because her congregation could not handle the Black Lives Matter movement, now works in information technology. The idea of going back into the ministry is still somewhat open to her, but she would not serve in a congregation. She would love to create something new with a group of clergywomen of color that is explicitly not a church. She says, "None of us want to be tied down to a mortgage or to property, but to do ministry in different ways and in different settings that meet people where they are." For her, ministry is about the relationships she builds with others ("meet people where they are") and not about a structure or organizations. She is discerning what a ministry without a structure could look like, but she has yet to find a way to build this new community.

The pattern of clergy leaving in order to find a deeper sense of community and connection reinforces what we found in our previous research with the Dechurched Project among laity who are "done" with church.[9] Laypeople are leaving congregations because they did not find authentic connections with others within the traditional church structure. Instead, they found judgment, bureaucracy, and institutional maintenance. Repeatedly, laypeople told us that their faith is deeply tied to relationships with others. As layperson Ella tells us, "I was kind of hoping to find a place where folks could be accepting of one another and actually do something with their faith and not just be the people who collect money and pay bills and get your sermon for the week and go home. That's not enough for me. I never found it in church, so when it appeared outside of the church, I jumped on it."[10] What our research on clergy tells us is that this pattern does not happen only for people in the pews. It is also occurring for those behind the pulpit. Clergy lead organizations meant to develop relationships and community—with God and with others. Yet these leaders find their congregations are not able to develop deeper communities or connections. They must search elsewhere for different models. Charles left the Presbyterian ministry so he could follow his calling to serve hurting teenagers. Peter found that authentic conversations happen at a storage facility and not within his church, and Brian is still searching for a model that can actually improve the lives of those on the streets.

SOCIAL AIRBAGS

Why do some pastors succeed when they transition out of the ministry, while others struggle to find new lives? In his research on middle-class and poor children, social scientist Robert Putnam offers the metaphor of "social air bags" to describe the varied resources that people draw on when encountering change or adversity.[11] Social airbags cushion and protect people who experience negative social events. They are the "financial, sociological, and institutional resources" that help soften the blow when a crisis occurs.[12] Social airbags could be an emergency savings fund, a well-connected friend, or a valued credential that can make weathering a major life transition easier.

One of the major differences between Brian and Peter, Charles, or Robert is Brian's lack of social airbags. When Peter needed to transition out of ministry, he and his wife were able to open a coffee shop. Even when the shop became untenable, he had the financial resources to take on a loan, which allowed him to take the job managing the storage facilities. Charles too had social airbags. He could afford the time and money to attend a three-day vocational workshop, and his bachelor's degree in psychology was a valid credential that did not carry the stigma of professional ministry. These social airbags softened the blow of leaving congregational ministry and were the resources that qualified him for his next career as a probation officer.

Robert's airbags were financial and relational. His wife had a well-paying medical career, so his family was not financially ruined when he left congregational work. He could even be a stay-at-home dad for a year. He also had well-connected friends who owned prime property and invited him to be a part of a new business venture. He then had the entrepreneurial know-how to start his own tea shop. Without this financial savvy, his powerful friends, or his wife's salary, his prospects would have been much dimmer.

Furthermore, all three of these former pastors worked in established and wealthy congregations, which means they were building social connections and financial resources even while working as pastors. To extend the metaphor, Charles, Peter, and Robert were installing their social airbags while in ministry, so when they left, they could be deployed to soften the blow of leaving.

Brian, however, had none of these social airbags. His congregation was small and underfunded. When he needed to earn more money in order for his ministry to survive, he could not find another middle-class job based on his Bible college degree in "pastoral studies," and he did not have a spouse with a high-paying career. Instead, he drove a taxi and was a freelance photographer, both tenuous jobs with low pay. While he did end up getting a job selling technology products, this current position is also low paying and does not connect with his calling to help the downtrodden.

As much as North Americans are hesitant to talk about it, social class matters. We can see this in the lives of these pastors who left the ministry. The pastors who had more resources built a cushion around their lives. Like the physical ones in cars, social airbags soften the blow of a major life event. Because being a pastor is a master status, leaving the profession can be a crisis.[13] Well-placed friendships, another source of family income, and the entrepreneurial skills to start a new business are all vitally important to making the transition as smooth as possible. Without these social airbags, the transition can produce a violent crash that inflicts major damage on a former pastor's financial, social, and spiritual life. This is what Brian experienced, and he is still recovering.

CONCLUSION

These pastors desperately want to be a part of a community that is authentic and relational, and they did not find such a community within their congregations. Instead, they had to discover how to build it—by having conversations while managing storage units, guiding teenagers as a probation officer, or selling tea that supports those leaving sex work. Guided by their calling and through hard work and some luck, they had to create avenues that led to deeper meanings in their ex-pastor lives. Yet the avenues these pastors found are not long-term institutions meant to build relationships and develop people's spirituality. The cultural models for ministry in North America do not offer many pathways that require spiritual leadership outside of the traditional congregational structure. We do not have a defined "career track" for seminary gradu-ates who do not want to serve as pastors of congregations or as chaplains but still feel called to strengthen communities and deepen people's relationships with God. Instead, the pastors we spoke to have had to creatively pioneer their ways so they could faithfully follow God's call.

THE TAKEAWAY

- Some pastors feel they must leave the ministry in order to follow God's calling on their lives.
- The role of a pastor is a "master status" that influences all other social roles, including careers.
- Former pastors often leave congregational minis-try because they are in search of careers that build deeper connections with others and more authentic communities.
- Some former pastors succeed in their new careers, able to connect with others and build strong communities. Others fail, unable to make the transition to meaning-ful, stable, and sustainable occupations.
- Social class matters in being successful in the transi-tion outside of ministry. Those with more resources have "social airbags" that can soften the blow of this major life change.

FOR REFLECTION AND DISCUSSION

For Pastors

- As a "master status," how does being a pastor influence your other social roles, such as a spouse, parent, or community member?
- How does congregational ministry align with your calling?
- Does your congregation ever get in the way of your calling? If so, how?
- How are you able to find deep connection and authentic community in your work? In what ways do you struggle to find these in your work?
- If you were to leave the ministry today, what resources (finances, relationships, skills, or credentials) would be your "social airbags" to help smooth this transition?

For Churches, Seminaries, and Denominations

- Does your pastor have a calling to a specific area of spiritual leadership? If so, what is it?
- Does the work your pastor carries out for your congregation fulfill his or her calling, or does this work get in the way?
- How can your organization create opportunities for pastors to experience deeper connections and authentic communities with others? How can that happen at the congregational, denominational, or seminary alumni level?
- Does your organization ever talk with former pastors to better understand why they left the ministry? If so, how could that information better equip current pastors for a healthier ministry?

CHAPTER 7
WHAT TO DO ABOUT BEING STUCK

> We are encouraged to live into the future by immersing ourselves in the best of our past, formed with a practical wisdom.
> —L. Gregory Jones and Andrew P. Hogue,
> *Navigating the Future*

These pastors feel stuck. Some have left the ministry and others remain. Yet each minister we spoke to was profoundly affected by the large and complex social forces of capitalism, social Darwinism, and secularization. The traditional way of being a pastor in a congregation can actually work well within a system built around social Darwinism and capitalism. Growth is the key metric of success, and congregations compete with one another for an increasing number of people. Historically, the combination of these two social forces was not necessarily problematic because people kept coming to church. In fact, sociologists Roger Finke and Rodney Stark show that *because* early America was capitalistic and Darwinist, North American religion had a strength and vibrancy to it that was not seen in Europe with its state churches.[1]

However, once we add secularization to the mixture, the pastoral role and the congregational form become more tenuous. Now there are fewer people to recruit, but the rules of the game still assume numerical growth. As a result, pastors are alienated from their own faith when they feel like they have to sell their spiritual lives in the marketplace to attract new members. If they do not "produce," they do not grow their membership. Congregations become bureaucratic and internally focused in this environment. They have to direct their energies to either managing a spirit-deadening bureaucracy or making sure their congregations on life support stay open. Pastors begin to wonder if congregations can continue to be places where they can fulfill their spiritual calling. In a secularizing world, the profession of the clergy is devalued because fewer people are in congregations. The few successful congregations do not employ the bulk of pastors. Most pastors will shepherd small congregations with few resources, and the status of clergy decreases.

And so pastors are left with a feeling of being stuck. They feel stuck in a calling that takes a passionate desire to serve God and reduces it to a commodity sold on the marketplace. They are stuck in congregations that are either dying or so focused on growth and performance that they have squeezed the Spirit out. And they are stuck in their careers because no employer knows what to do with a former pastor with an MDiv.

What are we who care passionately about creating a healthy and flourishing ministry to do about this situation? In his book on secularization and the growth of the nones, Ryan Burge, an American Baptist pastor and a political scientist, offers some wise advice on what to do about the increasing secularization of North America. He urges people worried about the future of the church to follow Reinhold Niebuhr's serenity prayer: "God grant me the serenity to accept the things I cannot change, the courage to change the things I can, and the wisdom to know the difference." Then Burge attaches one major addition: "and the data to know the difference."[2] The data show us that capitalism, social Darwinism, and secularization are not going away. No pastor or congregation can singlehandedly change these powerful social forces. They are woven too deeply into the cultural fabric of North America for any individual person or group to affect them.

TWO CHOICES IN THE FACE OF BEWILDERMENT

And yet many in the church feel as though we are at an impasse. We cannot change these social forces, but we also do not feel like we can work within them. Something has to change. L. Gregory Jones and Andrew P. Hogue describe this feeling as a sense of "bewilderment" in their book *Navigating the Future*; it is a sense of "disorientation, confusion, paralysis."[3] We are in a period of bewilderment. Pastors are disoriented because they sense that the models passed down to them no longer work. They are confused because the powerful calling they felt that led them into ministry is being overwhelmed by the logistics of running a congregation. They are paralyzed because their churches are hemorrhaging members and focused on survival instead of spiritual development.

Jones and Hogue state that people often turn to one of two choices in bewildering times: traditionalism or futurism.[4] When people choose to follow traditionalism in the face of bewilderment, they can dig in "attempting to do as we've always done out of habit, nostalgia, fear, or resistance to the idea of doing anything else."[5] A traditionalism within congregational ministry expects the old model to work: people will continue to be called into lifelong vocations of being pastors within healthy congregations with full pews. This was the model that Glen from chapter 4 entered into before he saw it unravel in his Presbyterian ministry. According to traditionalism, people who do not follow this path are thought to have failed somehow because the system is not broken. For them, the pathway is assumed to work. Yet the path of traditionalism leaves pastors stuck even further because it does not take seriously the impact of secularization on the life and work of congregational ministry. Pastors are working harder and seeing fewer results within the traditionalist model.

The other option in the face of bewilderment is futurism, which wants to destroy past models and create something new and exciting. In the words of Jones and Hogue, futurism wants to "disrupt, disrupt, disrupt."[6] In the context of congregational ministry, futurism argues it is the idea of the congregation itself that needs to be dismantled. Congregations no longer work because fewer people want to join them. Instead, futurism offers a vision of something new, whether it is book clubs, or supper clubs, or hiking clubs to help connect people with God and one another. Therefore, the profession of a pastor, as we currently know it, is no longer relevant either. To expect a congregation to support a full-time pastor is no longer a reasonable expectation, and so we should dismantle this model as well. If "pastor" is not a role that we should keep, then neither should we retain the MDiv or seminaries. All things related to the traditional concept of congregational ministry need to be demolished so that something new can be raised from their rubble.

The path of futurism also leaves pastors stuck, however, because it assumes that there is no wisdom to be found within the centuries-old pattern of congregations gathering together for worship and study. It assumes that sociological forces like culture and institutions are easily constructed in one generation and that pastors have the ability to create new, long-lasting wisdom from the ground up.

TRADITIONED INNOVATION

As an alternative to the two paths of traditionalism and futurism in the face of bewildering circumstances, we can use what Jones and Hogue call "traditioned innovation" as a guide.[7] Instead of digging in our heels to force the traditional congregational model to work or seeking to blow up the concept entirely, traditioned innovation offers us a way to look to the wisdom of the past in order to help us navigate a future that seems bewildering. They write, "Innovation can't be just about 'making things up' and starting from scratch. We believe that the innovation that matters is innovation that draws on the best of the past, carrying forward its wisdom."[8]

Using traditioned innovation, we cannot solve the problems that are facing pastors today. We cannot fill empty pews or remove the effects of capitalism on congregations. But we can look to the wisdom of the past to find ways to navigate an uncertain future and to create a faithful and flourishing ministry. To do this, we move beyond our training as sociologists who focus on measurable, empirical data and stretch ourselves toward a vision of future possibilities grounded in the Christian tradition. To be forthright, this is challenging for us. As sociologists, our training is in analyzing "what is" based on data and not in prescribing "what should be" based on theology and ethics. Yet I (Ferguson) will also use my experience as a pastor and my training in divinity school to offer ways forward to navigate the future. We will draw on Scripture, theology, and the sociological tradition to offer three major recommendations:

1. Understand relationships are layered.
2. Tell your story to undermine bureaucracy.
3. Close struggling congregations, knowing the Holy Spirit is still active in the church.

We wrote this book with three audiences in mind: clergy, the congregations and denominations who support these clergy, and the laity who would want to understand their own pastors better. Each of these recommendations is applicable to each group. Our goal is not to offer an exhaustible list of how to fix the experiences of being a "stuck pastor." Instead, it is to provide three examples of using the wisdom of the past so we can better create a flourishing clergy.

UNDERSTAND RELATIONSHIPS ARE LAYERED

One of the major sources of frustration that our stuck pastors consistently mentioned was the difficulty of finding authenticity within their congregations. This manifested itself in two ways. First, some of the pastors did not feel as though their own experiences in worship were authentic when they were leading services. As Evangelical pastor Peter says in chapter 1, "It just wasn't authentic. It wasn't real transformation. It was a job." A major part of their "job" was to stand in front of their congregations guiding people in worship. This, for some pastors, did not translate into authentic spiritual experiences. Second, other pastors struggled with authenticity because they were hesitant to reveal parts of themselves to their congregations. They felt like they had to present the perfect image of a pastor. As the Presbyterian pastor Charles notes in chapter 1, "You can't be yourself. You've got to be a superior person. You can't smoke. You can't cuss. . . . But you have to be this morally superior person, and that's a really bad dynamic."

What do we do about this "bad dynamic" of pastors struggling to be authentic with their congregations? The model of traditionalism would advocate that nothing changes. At some level, pastors *are* producing a product. They *are* on stage leading worship, and there *is* an expectation that pastors be morally superior. In the Bible, James 3:1 even says, "Not many of you should become teachers, my brothers and sisters, for you know that we who teach will be judged with greater strictness." The path of traditionalism would ask, Why should the expectations for pastors change just because an individual is struggling?

Futurism would see the whole model of congregational ministry as problematic. Congregations themselves are spaces of inauthenticity. Of course, no one can be spiritually perfect. The expectation that pastors never doubt, never cuss, or never fail is unreasonable. Furthermore, no one can lead worship, being mindful of all the logistics of leading a congregation, and still have an authentic spiritual experience. The whole profession is designed to be inauthentic, and so we should question the very existence of congregations and clergy.

Traditionalism does not fully listen to the legitimate experiences of pastors who say they are struggling to find authenticity. It fails to understand that, in an environment shaped by social Darwinism, a pastor who does not create a perfect "product" may lose members, which are becoming a scarcer resource. Futurism does not acknowledge that without leadership, institutions are not sustainable, and institutions are the means through which humans pass down religious faith from one generation to the next. The two extremes of traditionalism and futurism are not tenable.

But there is wisdom from the past that can guide us. The early sociologist Charles Cooley notes that people's relationships are often organized in layers.[9] People have some close, intense relationships, what Cooley calls "primary groups," but other relationships are more formal and less based in personal feelings.[10] These are "secondary groups." Primary groups are small, long-lasting relationships that are based in emotional connections, and they have an enormous impact on a person's identity. The most important primary group is one's family, but other groups can be primary as well. Secondary groups, however, are larger, often temporary, and most likely exist to achieve a goal. They are important, but their impact on one's identity is not as powerful. An example of a secondary group is a softball team or a class in school.

The issue of authenticity within the pastorate sometimes arises because there is not a clear separation between primary and secondary groups in congregations. The lines are blurred. Congregations are by nature secondary groups. They are large and have a specific purpose. Yet pastors are frequently expected to treat them as primary groups, filled with intense emotional connections. Similar to primary groups, a congregation can influence one's identity, and a pastor's own identity can be wrapped up in her or his role as the leader of that congregation.

In the biblical narrative, even Jesus's relationships form multiple layers. His close circle (or primary group) consists of his twelve disciples and then his followers. He has a more intimate and more vulnerable relationship with his disciples than with the crowd of followers. For instance, in Matthew 13, Jesus teaches the parables of the sower, weeds, and seeds to the crowd. Afterward, he has a more in-depth conversation with just his disciples about the meaning of these sayings, which he purposely does not share with the crowd. Later, in Matthew 26, he asks only his disciples to join him in the garden of Gethsemane to pray. He is scared because he is about to be arrested and executed, and so in an act of vulnerability, he says to his disciples, "My soul is overwhelmed with sorrow to the point of death. Stay here and keep watch with me" (Matt 26:38 NIV). Jesus acts differently with each relationship layer. He does not share everything with the crowd. They do not go with him into the garden of Gethsemane. Instead, he has a smaller group of more intimate friendships with whom he can be authentic.

There is wisdom here from both Scripture and the sociological tradition. People live within a multilayered web of relationships, only some of which are able to accommodate vulnerability and authenticity. Denominations, congregations, and clergy themselves need to work at honoring the multiple layers of relationships. Pastors must have the ability to authentically express who they are with others and to worship without the feeling that they are overseeing a production. Importantly, *this may not occur within their own congregations.* As clergy health psychologist Rae Jean Proeschold-Bell and theologian Jason Byassee write in their landmark book on clergy health, *Faithful and Fractured,* "Clergy are surrounded by people. However, we shouldn't confuse social interaction with supportive relationships. Clergy may interact with people all day, but that doesn't mean they're receiving support from others."[11]

Therefore, we recommend that clergy should participate in peer groups, groups with other clergy, where they can be honest, vulnerable, and authentic. They should have the freedom to express with others their doubts in faith or frustrations with congregational ministry. In short, they need to have a "safe space." They might meet with a clergy group once a month or participate in a quarterly clergy retreat. At these gatherings, there would be conversation and worship, but an important aspect of the gathering is that the clergy should not lead the worship service. They should not have to plan it or worry about logistics. This experience should not be a production for them. Instead, these gatherings should be places to connect with others and worship authentically.

Researchers have found that being a part of an authentic community is critical for clergy well-being. One of the major findings of the Duke Clergy Health Initiative, a long-term research project that explores all aspects of clergy well-being, is that the pastors who are the most satisfied with their careers and most feel like they are flourishing are those who are deeply embedded in meaningful relationships.[12] In an interview from that project, one pastor says, "My biggest thing is having someone to be accountable to. . . . I have a best friend because they don't take no stuff. . . . We're both pastors, so we know the day-to-day stresses and strains. We're able to relate."[13] Being within a community where one is able to be authentic can even affect how young clergy perceive their calling. I (Ferguson) conducted research into how seminarians transition into the clergy profession.[14] Those who felt a strong, accepting sense of community were much more likely to want to go into the ministry than those who were isolated while in seminary. An authentic community can even affect a pastor's physical health, like contributing to or reducing the chances of obesity. In another study I conducted, clergy who were involved in a support group with other pastors were much less likely to be obese.[15]

I (Ferguson) personally experienced the importance of authentic community while I was a pastor in Houston, Texas. I was a part of a group of friends who met each Monday night for dinner. Many of us were on staff at neighborhood churches, but others were laypeople who were members of these congregations. We rotated who cooked and hosted, but every Monday night, we gathered around a home-cooked meal and shared our lives. We spent hours being open and vulnerable with one another about our failures in the ministry or our frustrations in the faith. We celebrated accomplished dreams together. Eventually, we gave the group the not-very-creative name Monday Night Dinner, or MND for short. It was sacrosanct. No one missed MND. It was an amazing experience to be authentic with other Christians when our careers within our congregations did not always allow us this luxury. It created a "primary group" so that members of my congregation could remain a "secondary group." At work, I was Pastor Todd. At MND, I was just "Todd." I loved my time as a minister. I was not a "stuck pastor." Yet a large part of my satisfaction, I believe, is because I was able to be authentic with others outside my congregation.

Authenticity is a key aspect of a flourishing and healthy ministry. We do not have to ignore the cries for help from pastors who struggle to be authentic, as the traditionalist model would have, nor do we need to get rid of the clergy profession altogether and abandon congregations. Instead, by understanding that we live within multiple layers of relationships, we can have more reasonable expectations. Both clergy and their congregations should not assume that every relationship a minister has is to be one of vulnerability. They should also recognize that the worship services they lead may not be the time when pastors have profound spiritual experiences. Yet these opportunities for vulnerability and authenticity must be built into a pastor's life.

TELL YOUR STORY TO
UNDERMINE BUREAUCRACY

In chapter 3, we stated that many pastors felt like local congregations were no longer the places where ministry happens. This is a bold statement, and we grounded it within the concept of the "iron cage of congregations." Many congregations are so bureaucratized that pastors feel constrained—as if they were in a cage—from effectively being able to minister. Their congregations become focused on institutional maintenance or numerical growth, and spiritual matters become secondary. As Noah, the Baptist pastor, shared with us in chapter 3, "It seemed like the way we were doing church was providing a structure to keep an organization going, but there was never the time or the inclination to really share life in Christ." Iron cages are rigid, and the pastors we interviewed believed they no longer had the freedom to follow their calling within them. In our research on the dones in *Church Refugees*, the laity said the same thing as well. Bureaucracies are driving people from the church.[16]

Of course, bureaucracies exist for a reason within congregations. As stated in the introduction, there is a concentration effect occurring in North American religion because of secularization. Fewer people are attending churches, but the ones remaining belong to larger congregations. Bureaucratization is a natural outcome of these large organizations. Bureaucracies are efficient. They are remarkably valuable in helping organizations survive over the long term, which is an important achievement in a world marked by secularization. Yet as our pastors told us, something is not right when congregations are bureaucratized. When rules, regulations, and institutional maintenance thwart the efforts of ministry, the strengths of a bureaucracy become iron cages.

So how do we navigate a future where congregations struggle with the iron cage of bureaucracy—where the very thing that can help congregations survive is also the very thing that can get in the way of ministry? The model of traditionalism might tell frustrated pastors and laity that nothing needs to change because the bureaucracy is doing what it was designed to do: ensure survival. We want congregations to survive over the long term, and part of that survival depends on having order and structure. Bureaucracies are a necessary part of running an organization, even a congregation. A futurism approach would question why we need any structure at all. Proponents might ask, Couldn't Christians just gather together for worship, prayer, and study without any organizational system in place? We believe both approaches are misguided. We have to neither give up on the idea of an organized congregation nor ignore the frustrations of bureaucracies in order to undermine the iron cage.

There is wisdom from Scripture that can guide us. In the book of Galatians, Paul is frustrated that the churches in the region are adding new rules and regulations to their Christian faith. After Paul preaches the gospel to the churches of Galatia, new missionaries come in and add the requirement that new converts to Christianity must follow Jewish laws, like circumcision.[17] As a response, Paul writes his heated letter to help correct the situation: "I am astonished that you are so quickly deserting the one who called you" (Gal 1:6). Next, before he lays out the theological and biblical reasons for not adopting these new rules, Paul *tells his story*. He writes, "You have heard, no doubt, of my earlier life in Judaism. I was violently persecuting the church of God and was trying to destroy it" (Gal 1:13). He tells how he encountered Christ, changed his direction, and began preaching. He goes on to describe how he confronted Peter, who was tempted to add more regulations to the Christian faith. For Paul, the foundation for countering these new regulations was not a theological treatise but the story of how God changed him and why it matters.

While Paul's example of battling early Christianity's religious regulations does not exactly address the modern forces of bureaucratization, there is wisdom here. To tell one's story is powerful. In "church" language, we might call this "testimony." Jones and Hogue call it "traditioning."[18] Stories remind us where we came from and why we are here. They interpret our present situations and help shape our imaginations for future possibilities. As Jones and Hogue say, "Stories provide us with better vantage points and opportunities to see ourselves and our worlds, and they are instrumental in equipping us to navigate turbulent futures."[19] As we will see, they can help us battle the iron cage of bureaucracies.

Based on the wisdom of testimonies, we recommend that pastors and their congregations continually tell their stories. Stories undermine bureaucracy because *no one's story is about bureaucracy*. Pastors, by telling people about your calling, you are reminding them why you entered into the ministry in the first place. Like Charles from the previous chapter, many of the pastors we spoke to felt a mismatch between their calling and the work required of congregational ministry. Charles was called to reach out to the hurting and vulnerable and felt like he could not do that within his congregational work. Yet if a pastor who feels this mismatch can share her or his story with the congregation, possibilities open up. The imaginations of both the congregants and the pastor can be shaped by this story to creatively follow the call. This storytelling process will undermine the bureaucratic institutional maintenance because it will show how restrictive it truly can be.

Congregations must tell their stories as well. Every congregation has a story about why it was started, how it has changed over the years, and what its current mission is. These organizational stories are powerful. They can ground the church and keep it focused on its mission. In essence, these stories are myths—not false narratives but deeply true stories that shape a community's identity. In the handbook *Studying Congregations*, sociologist Nancy Ammerman shows that these congregations' myths are conveyed in three ways: (1) what congregations do, (2) what congregations make, and (3) the stories congregations tell.[20]

I (Ferguson) saw the power of storytelling within these three modes when my wife and I moved to Waco, Texas, for me to start graduate school. We joined a large congregation, Harris Creek Baptist Church, which had it written in its bylaws that it must hold an annual business meeting every January to go over the budget and the church's mission statement. At first, I thought this was just a stale piece of bureaucracy. I wondered, "Why must a church meet every January to reinforce its bureaucracy?" When our first January came, we realized that it was more than another administrative regulation.

The church created an entire event out of it: the Imagine Banquet. Instead of just reporting a budget to the congregation, the leaders rented out a local art house theater, served everyone dinner, and then retold the story of the congregation's past ("We started as the little church out in the cornfield in the mid-1800s . . .") and their plan for the future ("Next year, we hope to . . ."). The event was transformed from a bureaucratic requirement into a celebration of identity and purpose.

The congregation *did* something and *told* its story by hosting the Imagine Banquet, but it also reinforced the story with the *material objects it made*. Professionally created posters that lined the church hallways retold the congregation's commitments. While they were not narrative in form, they did communicate the church's guiding principles: to be local rather than global, to be deep rather than wide, to create instead of reproduce, to go outside instead of inside, and to prioritize devotion instead of doctrine. The Imagine Banquet and these posters had a remarkable effect because they undermined the bureaucratic forces of a large congregation. If a program or ministry event failed one year, it was removed from the next year's calendar. If a traditional "church" event did not fit the congregation's vision, it wasn't created. For instance, this congregation does not host a traditional vacation Bible school like many other congregations. It simply does not fit the vision the people want for the congregation. It went against their guiding principles by reproducing an event that other churches did remarkably well and by inviting people inside the building when their goal was to get church members to go outside of the building and to be active in the community.

The power of telling a pastor's or a congregation's story is an effective way to restrict the negative effects of the "iron cage." Bureaucracies will creep into an organization; it is almost inevitable. But by telling their stories, congregations and pastors can make sure that institutional maintenance is not the singular goal of the church. Instead, the focus remains on the congregation's mission as it is supported by the pastor's calling.

CLOSE STRUGGLING CONGREGATIONS, KNOWING THE HOLY SPIRIT IS STILL ACTIVE

The pastors in small and declining congregations are struggling. Christopher, the Lutheran pastor from chapter 4, shared with us that his small congregation could not pay a full salary, and so his wife and children moved to another community so she could find other work. He sadly tells us, "Right now, being a pastor is not going to be able to sustain us." Many pastors, especially in mainline Protestantism, are experiencing firsthand the effects of secularization. They are leading congregations with fewer resources and shrinking memberships. This is incredibly stressful.

Often, when we present our research to groups, the audience responds with distress and despair as well, especially if they are Christians. During the Q&A time after the presentations, we receive questions that go something like this: "If congregations are closing and pastors want to leave the ministry, is there any hope for the church?!" Questions like these are understandable. The simple facts are that fewer people are attending churches, many churches are shrinking, and some are closing. But we do not have to respond with despair to these facts. Wisdom from the past can help us navigate an uncertain future, one that is being dramatically altered by the forces of secularization.

In the Apostles' Creed, Christians proclaim in the same breath, "I believe in the Holy Spirit, the holy catholic church." These statements are not only next to each other in this ancient statement of faith, but they are also connected. To believe in the Holy Spirit is to also trust that the church is a reality. This wisdom is important in the face of secularization. As fewer people attend services and congregations shrink, Christians will continue to state their belief in the life of the church.

It is important to separate the congregation (or church, with a lowercase c) from the church universal. The church consists of all of those whom God has called in all times and all places—the *ekklesia* (Greek: "those called out"). The theological statement that God calls a group of people is important because to believe in the church universal is to believe in the Holy Spirit. It is from the work of the Holy Spirit that the church arises. As theologian Karl Barth states in his *Dogmatics in Outline*, "Woe to us, where we think we can speak of the Church without establishing it wholly on the work of the Holy Spirit. *Credo in Spiritum sanctum*, but not in the *Credo in ecclasiam*. I believe in the Holy Spirit, but not in the Church. Rather, I believe in the Holy Spirit, and therefore also in the existence of the Church, of the congregation."[21] For Barth, the church *is* because the Holy Spirit *is*. The church is the natural manifestation of the work of the Holy Spirit.

Barth's emphasis on the Holy Spirit is helpful for Christians experiencing the effects of secularization. One's ecclesiology must be grounded in the Holy Spirit, and Christians believe that the Holy Spirit is and will continue to be active in the world. To lose hope about the future of the church is to lose hope in the Holy Spirit. Similarly, to believe that the Holy Spirit is active means to believe that the church will remain.

Yet a robust ecclesiology grounded in the Holy Spirit does not fully negate the despair in people's questions about the future of the church or with pastors desperately asking if the church can sustain a professional ministry. The lowercase *c* church is in fact changing. Congregations are shrinking, operating with fewer resources, and sometimes even closing. As Glen in chapter 4 grieved with great nostalgia, the work of ministry has been getting harder and harder. Therefore, when people ask us authors pessimistic questions about the future of the church, we have a lot of empathy. People are worried because their beloved congregations are in trouble.

Will today's congregations change and even possibly die off? Yes, even if it happens over centuries. When we think of the local churches where Paul (the biblical writer), or Perpetua (the third-century martyr), or Augustine (the fourth-century theologian) worshipped, we understand they are gone. Neither the physical structures nor their cultural forms are around today. In one hundred years, many churches in North America will no longer be around either. The ones that remain will look and feel different too. Just because current churches are dying does not mean that the church itself is dying. To think it is, is to believe the Holy Spirit is dying.

Therefore, based on the wisdom that has been handed down to us within the Apostles' Creed, we recommend that struggling congregations close their doors. To allow a congregation to die is not to give up on the church but to trust that God continues to be at work in the world. Congregations naturally have life cycles: childhood, adolescence, adulthood, elderhood, and death.[22] Congregations within the "elderly" stage (or what the sociologist David O. Moberg calls "the institutional stage") will either die or restart the cycle with a type of rebirth.

Congregations with few resources or dwindling memberships cannot provide pastors with full salaries. Just as Christopher showed, congregations that do not pay their clergy full-time salaries place these pastors in precarious situations that often leave families distressed. Instead of struggling to bring about some kind of congregational rebirth, which is very difficult, congregations can close. They can pass on their resources to other congregations or other groups that are doing life-giving work in their communities. Members can join and offer their time, talent, and resources to strengthen other congregations. Denominations should create policies that favor having fewer—but better-paying—pastoral positions.

Other approaches are possible though. Some denominations, such as the United Methodist Church, have cooperative ministry agreements where multiple congregations share one ordained pastor. Laypeople have major leadership roles in running the day-to-day operations of the congregations. Others think that the future of pastoral ministry is part time. In his book *Part-Time Is Plenty*, G. Jeffrey MacDonald recommends that struggling congregations hire part-time clergy instead of offering full-time positions with benefits.[23] This option may work for some pastors, such as those who already have other satisfying careers. Yet many pastors want full-time careers, especially if they have families or have spent three or four years in seminary earning an MDiv. The part-time pastorate is difficult. As Jeff from chapter 3 describes his part-time ministry in two American Baptist congregations, "It's doing the same work for less money." His two congregations could no longer pay his salary, and so Jeff left the ministry because it was not sustainable.

Instead of expecting pastors to serve part time, we should be more assertive in pruning congregations that are no longer viable. To recommend this in a book is easy, but to enact it is extremely difficult. Congregations are places full of memories and emotions. They are the sites of people's most important life events, like baptisms, weddings, and funerals. Yet many, especially within mainline Protestantism, already understand that congregations will need to close.

There are excellent resources to guide congregations and their clergy in how to navigate these waters. Sociologist and Episcopal priest Gail Cafferata's book *The Last Pastor* weaves together her own experience closing the congregation she served with a study of over 130 pastors who also guided their own congregational endings.[24] While her analysis is sociological, her approach is ultimately pastoral. Cafferata offers practical advice on the best leadership styles and how to deal with conflict during a congregation's final stage. *Ending with Hope*, a contributed volume about closing churches, offers practical guidance for discerning whether a congregation should close and for walking through a congregation's final season.[25] It includes advice on how to sell a church building, maintain the congregation's historical records, and plan for the final worship service. Resources are available to enter into a "holy death" for a congregation, but now we need the courage to trust that the Holy Spirit continues to be active.

CONCLUSION

Being a pastor is among the highest and most honorable callings. The requirements of the role embody nearly every virtue: sacrifice, devotion, loyalty, hard work, humility, service, empathy, and others. We undertook this study, and wrote this book, because we were seeing far too many clergy struggling to hold on to these virtues, although not because they didn't believe in them or the profession. Rather, they were struggling simply because the way we have collectively constructed the profession of "pastor" is increasingly out of touch with the realities of the modern world.

While I (Ferguson) was serving as a pastor in a church, I took a short vacation to visit a dear friend and fellow pastor at his home on the East Coast. We spent long hours talking about our faith and doubts and about the joys and struggles of serving in churches. He was struggling with many of the same issues presented in this book, such as authenticity, alienation, and bureaucracy. I did not know it at the time, but he would soon "leave the ministry" in search of deeper connections and a more authentic community by becoming an entrepreneur. (He is not a participant in this study.) During one late-night conversation after we had been really wrestling with the concept of ministry, he sighed, smiled, and said, "People continue to be called."

My friend's short statement is powerful. People continue to feel a call to serve God. Regardless of the form the church takes, women and men experience a divine calling to lead others in faith. They are passionate about pursuing justice and seeking God. We see this in our study. Even though they were deeply frustrated, the pastors we interviewed repeatedly stated they felt a divine call to the pastorate. They just did not know how to faithfully follow this call when the current congregational structure and the existing models of ministry got in the way. To feel a calling means that the Holy Spirit is active, and therein lies the hope. If the Holy Spirit is alive, the church is alive as well.

We hope this book leads to deeper conversations about how the church can support those who feel called by God to be leaders. People desperately need religious guides. The mystery and complexity of living out one's faith are all but impossible to navigate without someone alongside you. In short, clergy remain as important as ever. Yet the shape this leadership takes and the context in which it occurs may look different in a world affected by the forces of secularization, social Darwinism, and capitalism. The future of North American congregations may seem tenuous, and therefore, the role of the pastor as we know it may also be uncertain. We can grieve this change. Yet people will continue to be called because the Holy Spirit continues to be active in the world. The church's form will probably be different. It may not look like what we think of as "church," but people will still gather around Christ to worship God, read Scripture, and seek justice. Our task, then, is to creatively and courageously listen to this call and follow the Spirit's direction, even in the midst of uncertainty.

THE TAKEAWAY

- In a world characterized by capitalism, social Darwinism, and secularization, pastors and congregations face a bewildering and uncertain future.
- When confronted with bewilderment, we often choose traditionalism or futurism.
- A third way, "traditioned innovation," can help us navigate a future by using the wisdom of the past to chart a way forward into an uncertain future.
- Using the wisdom from both the sociological and Christian traditions, we offer three recommendations to help clergy who feel stuck.
    - Understand relationships are layered.
    - Tell your story to undermine bureaucracy.
    - Close struggling congregations, knowing the Holy Spirit is still active.

FOR REFLECTION AND DISCUSSION

For Pastors
- How does the future of your ministry seem bewildering to you? What feels uncertain?
- Where do you see people or organizations recommend "traditionalism," hoping to change nothing about ministry or your congregation?
- Where do you see the model of futurism—people and groups who want to dismantle the entire system and start again?
- Do you have an outlet where you can be authentic with others that is outside your congregation?
- Where can you worship without planning the service or worrying about the logistics?

- When was the last time your congregation heard "your story"? How would this storytelling open up your congregation's imagination to counteract bureaucracy?
- Does your congregation need to close? Could you be the leader to guide the group toward a "holy death"?

For Churches, Seminaries, and Denominations
- Does the future of your organization feel bewildering or uncertain? How so?
- Where does the inertia of traditionalism or the haste of futurism show up in your group? Which model is stronger?
- What can you offer your clergy that opens up space for them to develop authentic relationships and worship services that they do not lead?
- What is your group's story? Do your people know it? How would your story undermine the iron cage of bureaucracy and open up people's imaginations for a healthy future?
- Are there congregations under your care that need to close? How can you guide them toward meaningful, sacred endings?

Acknowledgments

From Both of Us

To begin, we must share a heartfelt acknowledgment to the clergy in this study. In many cases, they took real risks in telling us things in interviews that would surely have gotten them fired if they said them to their congregations. We are always amazed and humbled to hear people's stories, often as they tell them for the first time, just minutes after meeting them. Work like this wouldn't exist without people like you. We hope we have done justice to your stories.

We would like to thank our editor, Beth Gaede, and the entire team at Fortress Press. As a publisher that connects the world of ministry with academia, we could not have found a more perfect fit for this book. Furthermore, we are grateful that Fortress has ventured more deeply into the world of the social sciences in order to better serve the church. Beth's guidance in the formation of this book made it a much better work that can hopefully help stuck pastors.

This book began as a conversation at the annual joint meeting of the Society for the Scientific Study of Religion and the Religious Research Association. We are thankful for these two societies, which gave us space each year to present our findings and gather helpful feedback to shape the research found in this book.

A special note of thanks is also due here to Dr. Ashleigh Hope, who helped collect the data for this project and gave shape to some of the original conversations around people who have one foot in and one foot out of the church world.

From Josh

I want to extend deeply felt gratitude to my coauthor, Todd Ferguson. I learned so much from working with him. People work in partnerships and coauthor things for a variety of reasons. The best among those is because your coauthor brings something to the project that you could never manufacture alone. I have been so fortunate to have had that experience here. In many ways, this project was simply a pile of data waiting for a pulse before Todd came along and breathed life into the project with his expertise as a sociologist and his heart as a former pastor. The book exists because of him and is made immeasurably better because of his insights and care, which both show so clearly through his writing.

My wife and partner, Megan, has been her normal, immensely supportive self throughout this project that I hope to never take for granted.

From Todd

Just as Josh said above, coauthors truly are gifts. I am honored to have Josh as a cowriter, a fellow scholar, and a friend. His leadership in the data collection phase and keen insights into the dynamics for stuck pastors made this book immensely richer.

I am deeply indebted to the Duke Clergy Health Initiative and their annual summer writing retreat. Led by the estimable Rae Jean Proeschold-Bell, this group of scholars provided the space and motivation to write and think deeply about clergy well-being. Thank you, Rae Jean, Celia Hybels, Glen

Milstein, Jia Yao, Josh Rash, Logan Tice, David Eagle, Erin Johnston, Anna Holleman, Jessica Choi, Sohail Muhammad, and the rest of this incredible research team.

I am also grateful to my colleagues at the University of Mary Hardin–Baylor (UMHB) for creating the space to write a book while being at a teaching-intensive university. The librarians Jennifer Batson, Shiloh Fulton, Teresa Buck, and Sandy Heller were instrumental in helping me find all the scholarship I needed for this project. John Vassar, Stephen Baldridge, and Rebecca Peterson cultivated a wonderful environment on our campus for professors to advance our scholarship. UMHB's 2020 Summer Research Grant allowed me to fund the technology and the childcare I needed so I had time to write.

Related to childcare, behind every researcher is someone doing the care work that allows the scholar to focus. This project would not have been written without the dedicated work of Ms. Angel, Ms. Gabriella, and the staff at Primrose School of Woodway. Thank you.

This project began while I was a graduate student in the Baylor University Department of Sociology. Thank you, Carson Mencken, Sharon Tate, and Kevin Dougherty for your leadership and training.

Finally, I am so grateful for my wife, Emma. Thank you for being immensely gracious as we both balanced marriage, raising Eliza and Henry, and working in our careers. I could not have done this without you, and I love you.

Appendix

Stuck: Exploring Alienation among Religious Professionals

Interview Guide

Before the tape recorder starts: "Thank you so much for agreeing to talk with me. I want to make sure that you know the procedure before I turn on the recorder. Once the recorder begins, I will not use your name for confidentiality reasons. You can feel free to use your name if you want to and to use anyone else's if you want to. As a reminder, we will be taking the steps outlined in the consent form to protect confidentiality."

Now start the recorder and speak the interview code (the last four digits of the phone number and the two-digit month of the birthday) from the demographic form.

"Thanks. I'm hoping that we can now move in to talking a little bit about your religious background."

Job Description and Duties

What is your official job title?

How did you come to this position? (Probe for full work history.)

What got you interested in church work in the first place?

Did you ever think that church work would be a lifelong vocation?

> If yes, when did that shift?

Would you say that you felt a calling to this line of
   work?
      If yes, can you describe what that means?
      If yes, do you still feel called to do ministry in
         general and church work in particular?
Describe your primary job duties. (Probe here and the next
   few questions about what kinds of religious products they
   are charged with producing.)
Is there a discrepancy between your official job description
   and what you actually end up doing on a day-to-day
   basis?
Is there a discrepancy between either of those and what you
   want to do or feel called to do?

"Thanks. That's really helpful. Now I'd like to ask you a few
questions about how your job affects your faith life."

Personal Faith Life

Tell me about an important spiritual or religious moment in
   your life.
Do you have those kinds of experiences often?
      If not, why do you think that is?
      If yes, (probe for an explanation about when,
         where, and how often those occur).
How would you describe your own faith: strong, average,
   weak?
      Why did you choose this answer?
Do you think it's hard for pastors to have authentic faith
   experiences, since you spend so much time trying to
   create those experiences for other people?
If you weren't busy on Sunday mornings, would you go to
   church?

> If yes, do you have a specific place in mind
> that you'd go to? (Probe for why that spe-
> cific place so we can identify the important
> characteristics.)
> If no, why not?

"Great. So now that I have a better understanding of your role, I'd like to move into a discussion about why you feel stuck in that position."

Professional Pastor

When we first contacted you for this interview, you indi-
cated that if it weren't your job to be a pastor, you
wouldn't go to church. (Alter based on conditions of
contact.) Explain that to me more.

What is it about your job that has you feeling disconnected
from your faith or the church?

What keeps you from taking a different position in this
church or another religious organization?

What would you do if you got fired tomorrow?

Do you have a plan for how to transition out of this job if
you had to?

If you're unhappy in this profession, what are the barriers for
you to take a job in a different line of work?

"Great, I'd just like to collect a little bit of background information from you. Can you fill out the demographic form?"
(Alternatively, ask the demographic questions verbally.)

"Well, I think that's all I have. I really appreciate your time.
Now that you have a pretty good sense of what I'm interested
in, is there anything you think I forgot to ask, or was there
something you wanted to say but didn't get a chance to?"

"One last thing, can you think of anyone else who is in a similar position and might be willing to talk with us?" (If yes, get name and contact information. If no, then leave a card and ask the respondent to contact us if they think of anyone.)

Notes

Preface

1 You can find more about Packard's work on the dechurched at https://dechurched.net/.

2 Josh Packard, *The Emerging Church: Religion at the Margins* (Boulder, CO: Lynne Rienner, 2012); Josh Packard and Ashleigh Hope, *Church Refugees: Sociologists Reveal Why People Are Done with Church but Not Their Faith* (Loveland, CO: Group, 2015).

3 In the social sciences, *positionality* refers to the identities—background and assumptions both acknowledged and unspoken—that a researcher brings to the field they are studying. With the recognition that no research can be purely objective, it is important to acknowledge the explicit or implicit biases that one brings to the research.

4 Mark Chaves, Shawna L. Anderson, and Allison Eagle, "National Congregations Study," cumulative data file and codebook, Duke University Department of Sociology, 2018.

5 John Cardinal O'Connor, "International Reunion of Priests: The Necessity of Continuing Formation for the Priest," Roman Curia, June 18, 1996, available at https://www.vatican.va/roman_curia/congregations/cclergy/documents/rc_con_cclergy_doc_18061996_intr_en.html.

6 In sociological analysis, the word *structure* means something more than simply organizational charts, polity, or hierarchies. It implies long-standing patterns of people and resources that are often not perceptible at the individual level. Sociological "structure" is often contrasted with "culture," which consists of the values, beliefs, and norms within a structure. One helpful metaphor is that of a Monopoly game. Structure would be the game board, the metal pieces, the money, and the plastic houses. Culture would be the rules of the game, like earning money when a player passes "Go."

7   Dean R. Hoge and Jacqueline E. Wenger, *Pastors in Transition: Why Clergy Leave Local Church Ministry* (Grand Rapids, MI: William B. Eerdmans, 2005).

8   Joshua Harris (@harrisjosh), "My heart is full of gratitude. I wish you could see all the messages people sent me after the announcement of my divorce. They are . . . ," Instagram photo, July 26, 2019, https://www.instagram.com/p/B0ZBrNLH2sl/.

9   Daniel C. Dennett, Linda LaScola, and Richard Dawkins, *Caught in the Pulpit: Leaving Belief Behind* (Durham, NC: Pitchstone, 2015).

10 Christopher Adams et al., "Clergy Burnout: A Comparison Study with Other Helping Professions," *Pastoral Psychology* 66, no. 2 (April 2017): 147–75, https://doi.org/10.1007/s11089-016-0722-4; Ronald S. Beebe, "Predicting Burnout, Conflict Management Style, and Turnover among Clergy," *Journal of Career Assessment* 15, no. 2 (May 1, 2007): 257–75, https://doi.org/10.1177/10690 72706298157; Bruce Gordon Epperly and Katherine Gould Epperly, *Feed the Fire! Avoiding Clergy Burnout* (Cleveland, OH: Pilgrim, 2008); William N. Grosch and David C. Olsen, "Clergy Burnout: An Integrative Approach," *Journal of Clinical Psychology* 56, no. 5 (May 1, 2000): 619–32, https://doi.org/10.1002/(SICI)1097-4679(200005) 56:5<619::AID-JCLP4>3.0.CO;2-2; Anne Jackson and Craig Groeschel, *Mad Church Disease: Overcoming the Burnout Epidemic* (Grand Rapids, MI: Zondervan, 2009); J. Fred Lehr, *Clergy Burnout: Recovering from the 70-Hour Work Week—and Other Self-Defeating Practices*, Prisms (Minneapolis: Fortress, 2006); Douglas W. Turton, *Clergy Burnout and Emotional Exhaustion: A Socio-psychological Study of Job Stress and Job Satisfaction* (Lewiston, NY: Edwin Mellen, 2010); Daniel Spaite and Debbie Salter Goodwin, *Time Bomb in the Church: Defusing Pastoral Burnout* (Kansas City, MO: Beacon Hill, 1999).

Introduction

1   All names in this book are pseudonyms to protect the participants' identities.

2   Jackson W. Carroll, *God's Potters: Pastoral Leadership and the Shaping of Congregations*, Pulpit & Pew (Grand Rapids, MI: William B. Eerdmans, 2006), 102.

3 "Mainline Protestants" are the Protestant denominations that
   are more theologically liberal than Evangelical Protestants. These
   denominations are associated with the National Council of Churches
   and include the Episcopal Church, the United Methodist Church, the
   Presbyterian Church (U.S.A.), the United Church of Christ, the Christian Church (Disciples of Christ), the Evangelical Lutheran Church
   of America, the American Baptist Churches, and the United
   Church of Canada. Robert D. Putnam and David E. Campbell,
   American Grace: How Religion Divides and Unites Us (New York:
   Simon & Schuster, 2010).
4 Margaret Harris, "A Special Case of Voluntary Associations? Towards a
   Theory of Congregational Organization," *British Journal of Sociology* 49,
   no. 4 (December 1, 1998): 602–18, https://doi.org/10.2307/591291.
5 Peter L. Berger, *The Sacred Canopy: Elements of a Sociological
   Theory of Religion* (New York: Anchor, 1967), 138.
6 Steve Bruce, *Secularization: In Defence of an Unfashionable Theory*
   (Oxford: Oxford University Press, 2011).
7 Ryan P. Burge, *The Nones: Where They Came From, Who They Are,
   and Where They Are Going* (Minneapolis: Fortress, 2021); Joseph O.
   Baker and Buster G. Smith, *American Secularism: Cultural Contours
   of Nonreligious Belief Systems* (New York: NYU Press, 2015).
8 Joel Thiessen and Sarah Wilkins-Laflamme, *None of the Above* (New
   York: NYU Press, 2020), 7–8; Burge, *Nones*, 28–29.
9 Tom W. Smith et al., "General Social Surveys, 1972–2018," machine-
   readable data file, NORC, 2018, https://gss.norc.org/.
10 Michael Lipka, "5 Facts about Religion in Canada," *Pew Research
   Center* (blog), July 1, 2019, https://www.pewresearch.org/fact-tank/
   2019/07/01/5-facts-about-religion-in-canada/.
11 David Voas and Mark Chaves, "Even Intense Religiosity Is Declining in the United States: Comment," *Sociological Science* 5 (November 15, 2018): 694–710, https://doi.org/10.15195/v5.a29; David
   Voas and Mark Chaves, "Is the United States a Counterexample to
   the Secularization Thesis?," *American Journal of Sociology* 121, no. 5
   (March 1, 2016): 1517–56, https://doi.org/10.1086/684202; Philip
   Schwadel, "Age, Period, and Cohort Effects on U.S. Religious Service Attendance: The Declining Impact of Sex, Southern Residence,
   and Catholic Affiliation," *Sociology of Religion* 71, no. 1 (April 1,
   2010): 2–24, https://doi.org/10.1093/socrel/srq005.

12 Mark Chaves, *American Religion: Contemporary Trends* (Princeton, NJ: Princeton University Press, 2011).

13 These are the authors' own calculations using data from Chaves, Anderson, and Eagle, "National Congregations Study."

14 Chaves, *American Religion*, 64.

15 C. Wright Mills, *The Sociological Imagination*, 40th anniversary ed. (New York: Oxford University Press, 2000), 5.

Chapter 1: The Pastoral Role and the Alienation of Faith

1 Karl Marx, "Economic and Philosophic Manuscripts of 1844," in *The Marx-Engels Reader*, ed. Robert C Tucker, 2nd ed. (New York: W. W. Norton, 1845), 66–125.

2 Marx, 70.

3 Marx, 74.

4 Arlie Russell Hochschild, *The Managed Heart: Commercialization of Human Feeling* (Berkeley: University of California Press, 2012), 7.

5 Hochschild, 19.

6 Hochschild, 194.

7 Hochschild, 196.

8 Hochschild, 192.

9 Roger Finke and Rodney Stark, *The Churching of America, 1776–2005: Winners and Losers in Our Religious Economy* (New Brunswick, NJ: Rutgers University Press, 1992).

10 Julie Ménard and Luc Brunet, "Authenticity and Well-Being in the Workplace: A Mediation Model," *Journal of Managerial Psychology* 26, no. 4 (January 1, 2011): 331–46, https://doi.org/10.1108/02683941111124854.

11 Antonio Ariza-Montes et al., "Authenticity and Subjective Wellbeing within the Context of a Religious Organization," *Frontiers in Psychology* 8 (2017): 3, https://doi.org/10.3389/fpsyg.2017.01228.

12 Alex M. Wood et al., "The Authentic Personality: A Theoretical and Empirical Conceptualization and the Development of the Authenticity Scale," *Journal of Counseling Psychology* 55, no. 3 (2008): 385–99, https://doi.org/10.1037/0022-0167.55.3.385.

13 Wood et al., 386.

14 Baker and Smith, *American Secularism*; Dennett, LaScola, and Dawkins, *Caught in the Pulpit*; Burge, *Nones*.

15 Darren E. Sherkat, *Changing Faith: The Dynamics and Consequences of Americans' Shifting Religious Identities* (New York: NYU Press, 2014); Darren E. Sherkat and John Wilson, "Preferences, Constraints, and Choices in Religious Markets: An Examination of Religious Switching and Apostasy," *Social Forces* 73, no. 3 (March 1, 1995): 993–1026, https://doi.org/10.1093/sf/73.3.993; Finke and Stark, *Churching of America*.

Chapter 2: Redefining a Calling

1 Cited in Carroll, *God's Potters*, 12.

2 Carroll.

3 H. Richard Niebuhr, *The Purpose of the Church and Its Ministry* (New York: Harper, 1956), 64.

4 Niebuhr, 64.

5 Robert N. Bellah et al., *Habits of the Heart: Individualism and Commitment in American Life* (Berkeley: University of California Press, 1985), 66.

6 Amy Wrzesniewski et al., "Jobs, Careers, and Callings: People's Relations to Their Work," *Journal of Research in Personality* 31, no. 1 (March 1, 1997): 21–33, https://doi.org/10.1006/jrpe.1997.2162; Richard Treadgold, "Transcendent Vocations: Their Relationship to Stress, Depression, and Clarity of Self-Concept," *Journal of Humanistic Psychology* 39, no. 1 (January 1, 1999): 81–105, https://doi.org/10.1177/0022167899391010; Ryan D. Duffy and Bryan J. Dik, "Research on Calling: What Have We Learned and Where Are We Going?," *Journal of Vocational Behavior* 83, no. 3 (December 1, 2013): 428–36, https://doi.org/10.1016/j.jvb.2013.06.006.

7 J. Stuart Bunderson and Jeffery A. Thompson, "The Call of the Wild: Zookeepers, Callings, and the Double-Edged Sword of Deeply Meaningful Work," *Administrative Science Quarterly* 54, no. 1 (2009): 32–57.

8 Bunderson and Thompson, 32.

9 Shoshana R. Dobrow and Jennifer Tosti-Kharas, "Listen to Your Heart? Calling and Receptivity to Career Advice," *Journal of Career Assessment* 20, no. 3 (August 1, 2012): 264–80, https://doi.org/10.1177/1069072711434412.

10 R. Stephen Warner, "The Place of the Congregation in the Contemporary American Religious Configuration," in *American Congregations*, vol. 2, *New Perspectives in the Study of Congregations*, ed. James P. Wind and James W. Lewis (Chicago: University of Chicago Press, 1994), 54–99.

11 Carroll, *God's Potters*; Wendy Cadge, *Paging God: Religion in the Halls of Medicine* (Chicago: University of Chicago Press, 2012).

12 Ann Swidler, "Culture in Action: Symbols and Strategies," *American Sociological Review* 51, no. 2 (April 1, 1986): 273–86, https://doi.org/10.2307/2095521.

13 Warner, "Religious Configuration"; Fenggang Yang and Helen Rose Ebaugh, "Transformations in New Immigrant Religions and Their Global Implications," *American Sociological Review* 66, no. 2 (April 1, 2001): 269–88, https://doi.org/10.2307/2657418.

14 Nancy Tatom Ammerman, *Sacred Stories, Spiritual Tribes: Finding Religion in Everyday Life* (New York: Oxford University Press, 2013).

15 Ammerman, 301.

16 Ammerman, 301.

17 Mark Chaves, *Congregations in America* (Cambridge, MA: Harvard University Press, 2004).

Chapter 3: The Congregation as Both a Community of Faith and a Business

1 Chaves.

2 Finke and Stark, *Churching of America*; Jon Butler, Grant Wacker, and Randall Balmer, *Religion in American Life: A Short History*, 2nd ed. (New York: Oxford University Press, 2011).

3 Paul J. DiMaggio and Walter W. Powell, "The Iron Cage Revisited: Institutional Isomorphism and Collective Rationality in Organizational Fields," *American Sociological Review* 48, no. 2 (April 1, 1983): 147–60, https://doi.org/10.2307/2095101.

4   John W. Meyer and Brian Rowan, "Institutionalized Organizations: Formal Structure as Myth and Ceremony," *American Journal of Sociology* 83, no. 2 (September 1, 1977): 340–63, https://doi.org/10 .1086/226550; Cathryn Johnson, Timothy J. Dowd, and Cecilia L. Ridgeway, "Legitimacy as a Social Process," *Annual Review of Sociology* 32, no. 1 (2006): 53–78, https://doi.org/10.1146/annurev.soc .32.061604.123101.

5   DiMaggio and Powell, "Iron Cage Revisited."

6   Voas and Chaves, "Secularization Thesis," 1517–56; Chaves, *Congregations in America.*

7   Meyer and Rowan, "Institutionalized Organizations."

8   Chaves, *Congregations in America.*

9   Max Weber, *Economy and Society* (Berkeley: University of California Press, 1978).

10   Max Weber, *The Protestant Ethic and the Spirit of Capitalism*, trans. Stephen Kalberg, rev. 1920 ed. (New York: Oxford University Press, 2011), 177.

11   Josh Packard and Todd W. Ferguson, "Being Done: Why People Leave the Church, but Not Their Faith," *Sociological Perspectives* 62, no. 4 (August 1, 2019): 499–517, https://doi.org/10.1177/0731121 418800270.

12   Packard and Ferguson; Packard and Hope, *Church Refugees.*

13   They are similar to but different from the "nones"—those who do not claim to associate with any religious tradition. The dones continue to say they are Christians.

14   Packard and Ferguson, "Being Done," 505.

Chapter 4: The Changing Riverbed

1   Chaves, *American Religion.*

2   "Southern Baptist Convention," Association of Religion Data Archives, accessed June 16, 2020, http://www.thearda.com/landing/sbc/.

3   The word *Evangelical* in many Lutheran denominations is often confusing. The word in the title does not mean a conservative religious orientation focused on individual conversion and biblical literalism. Instead, it comes from the biblical Greek word *euangelion*, meaning

"gospel." Therefore, a Lutheran denomination can have the word *Evangelical* in its title (e.g., the Evangelical Lutheran Church in America) but not be an Evangelical group.

4   Mark Wingfield, "SBC Loses Another 435,000 Members in 2020," *Baptist News Global*, May 24, 2021, https://baptistnews.com/article/ sbc-loses-another-435000-members-in-2020/; "Annual Church Profile Statistical Summary, 2019," Southern Baptist Convention, June 4, 2020, https://www.baptistpress.com/resource-library/news/ southern-baptist-convention-continues-statistical-decline-floyd-calls -for-rethinking-acp-process.

5   Dean M. Kelley, *Why Conservative Churches Are Growing: A Study in Sociology of Religion* (New York: Harper & Row, 1972).

6   Andrew Brown and Linda Woodhead, *That Was the Church That Was: How the Church of England Lost the English People* (London: Bloomsbury Continuum, 2016), 63.

7   Chaves, *American Religion*, 81–93.

8   Philip Jenkins, *Fertility and Faith: The Demographic Revolution and the Transformation of World Religions* (Waco, TX: Baylor University Press, 2020).

9   Michael Hout, Andrew Greeley, and Melissa J. Wilde, "The Demographic Imperative in Religious Change in the United States," *American Journal of Sociology* 107, no. 2 (September 1, 2001): 468–500.

10   Samuel L. Perry and Cyrus Schleifer, "Are the Faithful Becoming Less Fruitful? The Decline of Conservative Protestant Fertility and the Growing Importance of Religious Practice and Belief in Childbearing in the US," *Social Science Research* 78 (February 1, 2019): 137–55, https://doi.org/10.1016/j.ssresearch.2018.12.013.

11   Chaves, *American Religion*; Vern L. Bengston, *Families and Faith: How Religion Is Passed Down across Generations* (New York: Oxford University Press, 2013).

12   Putnam and Campbell, *American Grace*, 141.

13   Mark T. Mulder, Aida I. Ramos, and Gerardo Martí, *Latino Protestants in America: Growing and Diverse* (Lanham, MD: Rowman & Littlefield, 2017); "Changing Faiths: Latinos and the Transformation of American Religion," Pew Hispanic Center and Pew Forum on Religion and Public Life, April 25, 2007, https://www.pewforum .org/2007/04/25/changing-faiths-latinos-and-the-transformation-of -american-religion-2/.

14 Bengtson, *Families and Faith*; Jesse Smith, "Transmission of Faith in Families: The Influence of Religious Ideology," *Sociology of Religion* 82, no. 3 (2021): 332–56, https://doi.org/10.1093/socrel/sraa045.

15 Patricia Snell et al., "Denominational Differences in Congregation Youth Ministry Programs and Evidence of Systematic Non-response Biases," *Review of Religious Research* 51, no. 1 (2009): 21–38; Chaves, Anderson, and Eagle, "National Congregations Study"; Penny Edgell, *Religion and Family in a Changing Society* (Princeton, NJ: Princeton University Press, 2006).

16 H. Richard Niebuhr, *The Social Sources of Denominationalism* (Gloucester, MA: Peter Smith, 1929).

17 Chaves, *American Religion*.

18 Putnam and Campbell, *American Grace*; D. Michael Lindsay, *Faith in the Halls of Power: How Evangelicals Joined the American Elite* (New York: Oxford University Press, 2008).

19 Chaves, *American Religion*.

20 Putnam and Campbell, *American Grace*.

21 "Majority of Public Favors Same-Sex Marriage, but Divisions Persist," Pew Research Center, May 14, 2019, https://www.pewresearch.org/politics/2019/05/14/majority-of-public-favors-same-sex-marriage-but-divisions-persist/; "A Century after Women Gained the Right to Vote, Majority of Americans See Work to Do on Gender Equality," Pew Research Center, June 7, 2020, https://www.pewresearch.org/social-trends/2020/07/07/a-century-after-women-gained-the-right-to-vote-majority-of-americans-see-work-to-do-on-gender-equality/.

22 James Davison Hunter, *Culture Wars: The Struggle to Control the Family, Art, Education, Law, and Politics in America* (New York: Basic Books, 1992).

23 James K. Wellman, *Evangelical vs. Liberal: The Clash of Christian Cultures in the Pacific Northwest* (New York: Oxford University Press, 2008).

24 Christian Smith, *American Evangelicalism: Embattled and Thriving* (Chicago: University of Chicago Press, 1998); Rodney Stark and Roger Finke, *Acts of Faith: Explaining the Human Side of Religion* (Berkeley: University of California Press, 2000).

25 Laurence R. Iannaccone, "Why Strict Churches Are Strong," *American Journal of Sociology* 99, no. 5 (March 1, 1994): 1180–211, https://doi.org/10.1086/230409.

26 Smith, *American Evangelicalism.*
27 Michael K. Girlinghouse, *Embracing God's Future without Forgetting the Past: A Conversation about Loss, Grief, and Nostalgia in Congregational Life* (Minneapolis: Fortress, 2019).
28 Girlinghouse, vii–viii.

Chapter 5: Why Don't They Leave the Ministry?

1 Carroll, *God's Potters.*
2 Dennett, LaScola, and Dawkins, *Caught in the Pulpit.*
3 Megan Brenan, "Nurses Again Outpace Other Professions for Honesty, Ethics," Gallup.com, December 20, 2018, https://news.gallup.com/poll/245597/nurses-again-outpace-professions-honesty-ethics.aspx; R. J. Reinhart, "Nurses Continue to Rate Highest in Honesty, Ethics," Gallup.com, January 6, 2020, https://news.gallup.com/poll/274673/nurses-continue-rate-highest-honesty-ethics.aspx.
4 Associated Press / NORC, "Attitudes toward Clergy and Religious Leadership," AP NORC, May 2019, http://www.apnorc.org:80/projects/Pages/Attitudes-toward-Clergy-and-Religious-Leadership.aspx.
5 Chaves, *American Religion.*
6 Anti-Defamation League, "Religious Accommodation in the Workplace: Your Rights and Obligations," July 29, 2015, https://www.adl.org/sites/default/files/documents/assets/pdf/civil-rights/religiousfreedom/religiousaccomodworkplace/religiousaccommodwkplacerevised07-29-15.pdf.
7 Erving Goffman, *Stigma: Notes on the Management of Spoiled Identity* (New York: Simon & Schuster, 1963), 3.
8 "Occupational Employment and Wage Statistics: Clergy," US Bureau of Labor Statistics, 2021, https://www.bls.gov/oes/current/oes212011.htm.
9 Packard and Ferguson, "Being Done," 499–517.
10 Teresa A. Sullivan, Elizabeth Warren, and Jay Lawrence Westbrook, *The Fragile Middle Class: Americans in Debt* (New Haven, CT: Yale University Press, 2020).
11 Alissa Quart, *Squeezed: Why Our Families Can't Afford America* (New York: HarperCollins, 2018).

Chapter 6: Leaving the Ministry to Follow the Call

1   Kristin Stewart, "Keeping Your Pastor: An Emerging Challenge," *Journal for the Liberal Arts and Sciences* 13, no. 3 (2009): 112; Randy Kanipe, "Guest Columnist: Clergy Killers Are a Problem for Our Churches Everywhere," *Wesleyan Christian Advocate* (blog), October 29, 2007, http://wesleyanchristianadvocate.blogspot.com/2007/10/guest-columnist-clergy-killers-are.html.

2   Todd W. Ferguson, "Failing to Master Divinity: How Institutional Type, Financial Debt, Community Acceptance, and Gender Affect Seminary Graduates' Career Choices," *Review of Religious Research* 57, no. 3 (2015): 341–63, https://doi.org/10.1007/s13644-015-0209-2.

3   Allison Hamm and David Eagle, "Clergy Who Leave Congregational Ministry: A Review of the Literature," *Journal of Psychology and Theology*, April 24, 2021, https://doi.org/10.31235/osf.io/me4vd.

4   Hoge and Wenger, *Pastors in Transition.*

5   Hoge and Wenger, 198.

6   Everett Cherrington Hughes, "Dilemmas and Contradictions of Status," *American Journal of Sociology* 50, no. 5 (1945): 353–59.

7   Helen Rose Fuchs Ebaugh, *Becoming an Ex: The Process of Role Exit* (Chicago: University of Chicago Press, 1988).

8   Peter Harry Ballis, *Leaving the Adventist Ministry: A Study of the Process of Exiting* (Westport, CT: Greenwood, 1999).

9   Packard and Ferguson, "Being Done," 499–517; Packard and Hope, *Church Refugees.*

10   Packard and Ferguson, "Being Done," 509.

11   Robert D. Putnam, *Our Kids: The American Dream in Crisis* (New York: Simon & Schuster, 2015), 210.

12   Putnam, 198.

13   Ballis, *Leaving the Adventist Ministry.*

Chapter 7: What to Do About Being Stuck

1   Finke and Stark, *Churching of America.*

2   Burge, *Nones*, 128.

3   L. Gregory Jones and Andrew P. Hogue, *Navigating the Future: Traditioned Innovation for Wilder Seas* (Nashville: Abingdon, 2021), 47.

4   Jones and Hogue, 48.

5   Jones and Hogue, 48.

6   Jones and Hogue, 48.

7   Jones and Hogue.

8   Jones and Hogue, xviii.

9   Charles Horton Cooley, *Social Organization: A Study of the Larger Mind* (New York: Routledge, 2017), https://doi.org/10.4324/9781315129655.

10 Cooley.

11 Rae Jean Proeschold-Bell and Jason Byassee, *Faithful and Fractured* (Grand Rapids, MI: Baker Academic, 2018), 128.

12 Proeschold-Bell and Byassee, 127–29.

13 Proeschold-Bell and Byassee, 128.

14 Ferguson, "Failing to Master Divinity," 341–63.

15 Todd W. Ferguson et al., "Occupational Conditions, Self-Care, and Obesity among Clergy in the United States," *Social Science Research* 49 (January 2015): 249–63, https://doi.org/10.1016/j.ssresearch.2014.08.014.

16 Packard and Hope, *Church Refugees*; Packard and Ferguson, "Being Done," 499–517.

17 Richard B. Hays, *The Letter to the Galatians: Introduction, Commentary, and Reflections*, vol. 11 of *The New Interpreter's Bible* (Nashville: Abingdon, 2000).

18 Jones and Hogue, *Navigating the Future*, 119–46.

19 Jones and Hogue, 121.

20 Nancy T. Ammerman, "Culture and Identity in the Congregation," in *Studying Congregations: A New Handbook*, ed. Nancy Ammerman et al. (Nashville: Abingdon, 1998), 78–104; Studying Congregations website, accessed July 30, 2021, https://studyingcongregations.org/.

21 Karl Barth, *Dogmatics in Outline* (New York: Harper Torchbooks, 1959), 142.

22 David O. Moberg, *The Church as a Social Institution: The Sociology of American Religion*, 2nd ed. (Grand Rapids, MI: Baker, 1984), 118–24; Kevin D. Dougherty, Jared Maier, and Brian Vander Lugt, "When the Final Bell Tolls: Patterns of Church Closings in Two Protestant Denominations," *Review of Religious Research* 50, no. 1 (2008): 49–73.

23 G. Jeffrey MacDonald, *Part-Time Is Plenty: Thriving without Full-Time Clergy* (Louisville, KY: Westminster John Knox, 2020).

24 Gail Cafferata, *The Last Pastor* (Louisville, KY: Westminster John Knox, 2020).

25 Beth Ann Gaede, ed., *Ending with Hope: A Resource for Closing Congregations* (Lanham, MD: Rowman & Littlefield, 2002).

Bibliography

Adams, Christopher, Holly Hough, Rae Proeschold-Bell, Jia Yao, and Melanie Kolkin. "Clergy Burnout: A Comparison Study with Other Helping Professions." *Pastoral Psychology* 66, no. 2 (April 2017): 147–175. https://doi.org/10.1007/s11089-016-0722-4.

Ammerman, Nancy Tatom. "Culture and Identity in the Congregation." In *Studying Congregations: A New Handbook*, edited by Nancy Ammerman, Jackson Carroll, Carl Dudley, and William McKinney, 78–104. Nashville: Abingdon, 1998.

———. *Sacred Stories, Spiritual Tribes: Finding Religion in Everyday Life*. New York: Oxford University Press, 2013.

Anti-Defamation League. "Religious Accommodation in the Workplace: Your Rights and Obligations." July 29, 2015. https://www.adl.org/sites/default/files/documents/assets/pdf/civil-rights/religiousfreedom/religiousaccomodworkplace/religiousaccommodwkplacerevised07-29-15.pdf.

Ariza-Montes, Antonio, Gabriele Giorgi, Antonio Leal-Rodríguez, and Jesús Ramírez-Sobrino. "Authenticity and Subjective Wellbeing within the Context of a Religious Organization." *Frontiers in Psychology* 8 (2017). https://doi.org/10.3389/fpsyg.2017.01228.

Associated Press / NORC. "Attitudes toward Clergy and Religious Leadership." AP NORC. May 2019. http://www.apnorc.org:80/projects/Pages/Attitudes-toward-Clergy-and-Religious-Leadership.aspx.

Association of Religion Data Archives. "Southern Baptist Convention." Accessed June 16, 2020. http://www.the arda.com/landing/sbc/.

Baker, Joseph O., and Buster G. Smith. *American Secularism: Cultural Contours of Nonreligious Belief Systems*. New York: NYU Press, 2015.

Ballis, Peter Harry. *Leaving the Adventist Ministry: A Study of the Process of Exiting*. Westport, CT: Greenwood, 1999.

Barth, Karl. *Dogmatics in Outline*. New York: Harper Torchbooks, 1959.

Beebe, Ronald S. "Predicting Burnout, Conflict Management Style, and Turnover among Clergy." *Journal of Career Assessment* 15, no. 2 (May 1, 2007): 257–275. https://doi .org/10.1177/1069072706298157.

Bellah, Robert N., Richard Madsen, William M. Sullivan, Ann Swidler, and Steven M. Tipton. *Habits of the Heart: Individualism and Commitment in American Life*. Berkeley: University of California Press, 1985.

Bengtson, Vern L. *Families and Faith: How Religion Is Passed Down across Generations*. New York: Oxford University Press, 2013.

Berger, Peter L. *The Sacred Canopy: Elements of a Sociological Theory of Religion*. New York: Anchor, 1967.

Brenan, Megan. "Nurses Again Outpace Other Professions for Honesty, Ethics." Gallup.com, December 20, 2018. https://news.gallup.com/poll/245597/nurses-again -outpace-professions-honesty-ethics.aspx.

Brown, Andrew, and Linda Woodhead. *That Was the Church That Was: How the Church of England Lost the English People*. London: Bloomsbury Continuum, 2016.

Bruce, Steve. *Secularization: In Defence of an Unfashionable Theory*. Oxford: Oxford University Press, 2011.

Bunderson, J. Stuart, and Jeffery A. Thompson. "The Call of the Wild: Zookeepers, Callings, and the Double-Edged Sword of Deeply Meaningful Work." *Administrative Science Quarterly* 54, no. 1 (2009): 32–57.

Burge, Ryan P. *The Nones: Where They Came From, Who They Are, and Where They Are Going*. Minneapolis: Fortress, 2021.

Butler, Jon, Grant Wacker, and Randall Balmer. *Religion in American Life: A Short History*. 2nd ed. New York: Oxford University Press, 2011.

Cadge, Wendy. *Paging God: Religion in the Halls of Medicine*. Chicago: University of Chicago Press, 2012.

Cafferata, Gail. *The Last Pastor*. Louisville, KY: Westminster John Knox, 2020.

Carroll, Jackson W. *God's Potters: Pastoral Leadership and the Shaping of Congregations*. Pulpit & Pew. Grand Rapids, MI: William B. Eerdmans, 2006.

Chaves, Mark. *American Religion: Contemporary Trends*. Princeton, NJ: Princeton University Press, 2011.

———. *Congregations in America*. Cambridge, MA: Harvard University Press, 2004.

Chaves, Mark, Shawna L. Anderson, and Allison Eagle. "National Congregations Study." Cumulative data file and codebook. Duke University Department of Sociology, 2018.

Cooley, Charles Horton. *Social Organization: A Study of the Larger Mind*. New York: Routledge, 2017.

Dennett, Daniel C., Linda LaScola, and Richard Dawkins. *Caught in the Pulpit: Leaving Belief Behind*. Durham, NC: Pitchstone, 2015.

DiMaggio, Paul J., and Walter W. Powell. "The Iron Cage Revisited: Institutional Isomorphism and Collective

Rationality in Organizational Fields." *American Sociological Review* 48, no. 2 (April 1, 1983): 147–160. https://doi.org/10.2307/2095101.

Dobrow, Shoshana R., and Jennifer Tosti-Kharas. "Listen to Your Heart? Calling and Receptivity to Career Advice." *Journal of Career Assessment* 20, no. 3 (August 1, 2012): 264–280. https://doi.org/10.1177/1069072711434412.

Dougherty, Kevin D., Jared Maier, and Brian Vander Lugt. "When the Final Bell Tolls: Patterns of Church Closings in Two Protestant Denominations." *Review of Religious Research* 50, no. 1 (2008): 49–73.

Duffy, Ryan D., and Bryan J. Dik. "Research on Calling: What Have We Learned and Where Are We Going?" *Journal of Vocational Behavior* 83, no. 3 (December 1, 2013): 428–436. https://doi.org/10.1016/j.jvb.2013.06.006.

Ebaugh, Helen Rose Fuchs. *Becoming an Ex: The Process of Role Exit.* Chicago: University of Chicago Press, 1988.

Edgell, Penny. *Religion and Family in a Changing Society.* Princeton, NJ: Princeton University Press, 2006.

Emerson, Ralph Waldo. *The Journals and Miscellaneous Notebooks of Ralph Waldo Emerson.* Cambridge, MA: Harvard University Press, 1964.

Epperly, Bruce Gordon, and Katherine Gould Epperly. *Feed the Fire! Avoiding Clergy Burnout.* Cleveland, OH: Pilgrim, 2008.

Ferguson, Todd W. "Failing to Master Divinity: How Institutional Type, Financial Debt, Community Acceptance, and Gender Affect Seminary Graduates' Career Choices." *Review of Religious Research* 57, no. 3 (2015): 341–363. https://doi.org/10.1007/s13644-015-0209-2.

Ferguson, Todd W., Brita Andercheck, Joshua C. Tom, Brandon C. Martinez, and Samuel Stroope. "Occupational Conditions, Self-Care, and Obesity among Clergy in the

United States." *Social Science Research* 49 (January 2015): 249–263. https://doi.org/10.1016/j.ssresearch.2014.08.014.

Finke, Roger, and Rodney Stark. *The Churching of America, 1776–2005: Winners and Losers in Our Religious Economy.* New Brunswick, NJ: Rutgers University Press, 1992.

Gaede, Beth. *Ending with Hope: A Resource for Closing Congregations.* Bethesda, MD: Alban, 2002.

Girlinghouse, Michael K. *Embracing God's Future without Forgetting the Past: A Conversation about Loss, Grief, and Nostalgia in Congregational Life.* Minneapolis: Fortress, 2019.

Goffman, Erving. *Stigma: Notes on the Management of Spoiled Identity.* New York: Simon & Schuster, 1963.

Grosch, William N., and David C. Olsen. "Clergy Burnout: An Integrative Approach." *Journal of Clinical Psychology* 56, no. 5 (May 1, 2000): 619–632. https://doi.org/10.1002/(SICI)1097-4679(200005)56:5<619::AID-JCLP4>3.0 .CO;2-2.

Hamm, Allison, and David Eagle. "Clergy Who Leave Congregational Ministry: A Review of the Literature." *Journal of Psychology and Theology*, April 24, 2021. https://doi.org/ 10.31235/osf.io/me4vd.

Harris, Joshua (@harrisjosh). "My heart is full of gratitude. I wish you could see all the messages people sent me after the announcement of my divorce. They are. . . ." Instagram photo, July 26, 2019. https://www.instagram .com/p/B0ZBrNLH2sl/.

Harris, Margaret. "A Special Case of Voluntary Associations? Towards a Theory of Congregational Organization." *British Journal of Sociology* 49, no. 4 (December 1, 1998): 602–618. https://doi.org/10.2307/591291.

Hays, Richard B. *The Letter to the Galatians: Introduction, Commentary, and Reflections.* Vol. 11 of *The New Interpreter's Bible.* Nashville: Abingdon, 2000.

Hochschild, Arlie Russell. *The Managed Heart: Commercialization of Human Feeling*. Berkeley: University of California Press, 2012.

Hoge, Dean R., and Jacqueline E. Wenger. *Pastors in Transition: Why Clergy Leave Local Church Ministry*. Grand Rapids, MI: William B. Eerdmans, 2005.

Hout, Michael, Andrew Greeley, and Melissa J. Wilde. "The Demographic Imperative in Religious Change in the United States." *American Journal of Sociology* 107, no. 2 (September 1, 2001): 468–500.

Hughes, Everett Cherrington. "Dilemmas and Contradictions of Status." *American Journal of Sociology* 50, no. 5 (1945): 353–359.

Hunter, James Davison. *Culture Wars: The Struggle to Control the Family, Art, Education, Law, and Politics in America*. New York: Basic Books, 1992.

Iannaccone, Laurence R. "Why Strict Churches Are Strong." *American Journal of Sociology* 99, no. 5 (March 1, 1994): 1180–1211. https://doi.org/10.1086/230409.

Jackson, Anne, and Craig Groeschel. *Mad Church Disease: Overcoming the Burnout Epidemic*. Grand Rapids, MI: Zondervan, 2009.

Jenkins, Philip. *Fertility and Faith: The Demographic Revolution and the Transformation of World Religions*. Waco, TX: Baylor University Press, 2020.

Johnson, Cathryn, Timothy J. Dowd, and Cecilia L. Ridgeway. "Legitimacy as a Social Process." *Annual Review of Sociology* 32, no. 1 (2006): 53–78. https://doi.org/10.1146/annurev.soc.32.061604.123101.

Jones, L. Gregory, and Andrew P. Hogue. *Navigating the Future: Traditioned Innovation for Wilder Seas*. Nashville: Abingdon, 2021.

Kanipe, Randy. "Guest Columnist: Clergy Killers Are a Problem for Our Churches Everywhere." *Wesleyan Christian Advocate* (blog), October 29, 2007. http://wesleyan christianadvocate.blogspot.com/2007/10/guest-columnist -clergy-killers-are.html.

Kelley, Dean M. *Why Conservative Churches Are Growing: A Study in Sociology of Religion*. New York: Harper & Row, 1972.

Lehr, J. Fred. *Clergy Burnout: Recovering from the 70-Hour Work Week—and Other Self-Defeating Practices*. Prisms. Minneapolis: Fortress, 2006.

Lindsay, D. Michael. *Faith in the Halls of Power: How Evangelicals Joined the American Elite*. New York: Oxford University Press, 2008.

Lipka, Michael. "5 Facts about Religion in Canada." *Pew Research Center* (blog), July 1, 2019. https://www .pewresearch.org/fact-tank/2019/07/01/5-facts-about -religion-in-canada/.

MacDonald, G. Jeffrey. *Part-Time Is Plenty: Thriving without Full-Time Clergy*. Louisville, KY: Westminster John Knox, 2020.

Marx, Karl. "Economic and Philosophic Manuscripts of 1844." In *The Marx-Engels Reader*, edited by Robert C. Tucker, 2nd ed., 66–125. New York: W. W. Norton, 1845.

Ménard, Julie, and Luc Brunet. "Authenticity and Well-Being in the Workplace: A Mediation Model." *Journal of Managerial Psychology* 26, no. 4 (January 1, 2011): 331–346. https://doi.org/10.1108/02683941111124854.

Meyer, John W., and Brian Rowan. "Institutionalized Organizations: Formal Structure as Myth and Ceremony." *American Journal of Sociology* 83, no. 2 (September 1, 1977): 340–363. https://doi.org/10.1086/226550.

Mills, C. Wright. *The Sociological Imagination*. 40th anniversary ed. New York: Oxford University Press, 2000.

Moberg, David O. *The Church as a Social Institution: The Sociology of American Religion*. 2nd ed. Grand Rapids, MI: Baker, 1984.

Mulder, Mark T., Aida I. Ramos, and Gerardo Martí. *Latino Protestants in America: Growing and Diverse*. Lanham, MD: Rowman & Littlefield, 2017.

Niebuhr, H. Richard. *The Purpose of the Church and Its Ministry*. New York: Harper, 1956.

———. *The Social Sources of Denominationalism*. Gloucester, MA: Peter Smith, 1929.

O'Connor, John Cardinal. "International Reunion of Priests: The Necessity of Continuing Formation for the Priest." Roman Curia, June 18, 1996. https://www.vatican.va/roman_curia/congregations/cclergy/documents/rc_con_cclergy_doc_18061996_intr_en.html.

O'Dea, Thomas F., and J. Milton Yinger. "Five Dilemmas in the Institutionalization of Religion." *Journal for the Scientific Study of Religion* 1, no. 1 (1961): 30–41. https://doi.org/10.2307/1385174.

Packard, Josh. *The Emerging Church: Religion at the Margins*. Boulder, CO: Lynne Rienner, 2012.

Packard, Josh, and Todd W. Ferguson. "Being Done: Why People Leave the Church, but Not Their Faith." *Sociological Perspectives* 62, no. 4 (August 1, 2019): 499–517. https://doi.org/10.1177/0731121418800270.

Packard, Josh, and Ashleigh Hope. *Church Refugees: Sociologists Reveal Why People Are Done with Church but Not Their Faith*. Loveland, CO: Group, 2015.

Perry, Samuel L., and Cyrus Schleifer. "Are the Faithful Becoming Less Fruitful? The Decline of Conservative Protestant Fertility and the Growing Importance of Religious

Practice and Belief in Childbearing in the US." *Social Science Research* 78 (February 1, 2019): 137–155. https://doi .org/10.1016/j.ssresearch.2018.12.013.

Pew Hispanic Center and Pew Forum on Religion and Public Life. "Changing Faiths: Latinos and the Transformation of American Religion." April 25, 2007. https://www .pewforum.org/2007/04/25/changing-faiths-latinos-and -the-transformation-of-american-religion-2/.

Pew Research Center. "A Century after Women Gained the Right to Vote, Majority of Americans See Work to Do on Gender Equality." June 7, 2020. https://www.pewresearch .org/social-trends/2020/07/07/a-century-after-women -gained-the-right-to-vote-majority-of-americans-see-work -to-do-on-gender-equality/.

———. "Majority of Public Favors Same-Sex Marriage, but Divisions Persist." May 14, 2019. https://www.pew research.org/politics/2019/05/14/majority-of-public -favors-same-sex-marriage-but-divisions-persist/.

Proeschold-Bell, Rae Jean, and Jason Byassee. *Faithful and Fractured*. Grand Rapids, MI: Baker Academic, 2018.

Putnam, Robert D. *Our Kids: The American Dream in Crisis*. New York: Simon & Schuster, 2015.

Putnam, Robert D., and David E. Campbell. *American Grace: How Religion Divides and Unites Us*. New York: Simon & Schuster, 2010.

Quart, Alissa. *Squeezed: Why Our Families Can't Afford America*. New York: HarperCollins, 2018.

Reinhart, R. J. "Nurses Continue to Rate Highest in Honesty, Ethics." Gallup.com, January 6, 2020. https://news.gallup .com/poll/274673/nurses-continue-rate-highest-honesty -ethics.aspx.

Schwadel, Philip. "Age, Period, and Cohort Effects on U.S. Religious Service Attendance: The Declining Impact of

Sex, Southern Residence, and Catholic Affiliation." *Sociology of Religion* 71, no. 1 (April 1, 2010): 2–24. https://doi.org/10.1093/socrel/srq005.

Sherkat, Darren E. *Changing Faith: The Dynamics and Consequences of Americans' Shifting Religious Identities.* New York: NYU Press, 2014.

Sherkat, Darren E., and John Wilson. "Preferences, Constraints, and Choices in Religious Markets: An Examination of Religious Switching and Apostasy." *Social Forces* 73, no. 3 (March 1, 1995): 993–1026. https://doi.org/10.1093/sf/73.3.993.

Smith, Christian. *American Evangelicalism: Embattled and Thriving.* Chicago: University of Chicago Press, 1998.

Smith, Jesse. "Transmission of Faith in Families: The Influence of Religious Ideology." *Sociology of Religion* 82, no. 3 (2021): 332–356. https://doi.org/10.1093/socrel/sraa045.

Smith, Tom W., Michael Davern, Jeremy Freese, and Michael Hout. "General Social Surveys, 1972–2018." Machine-readable data file. NORC, 2018. https://gss.norc.org/.

Snell, Patricia, Christian Smith, Carlos Tavares, and Kari Christoffersen. "Denominational Differences in Congregation Youth Ministry Programs and Evidence of Systematic Non-response Biases." *Review of Religious Research* 51, no. 1 (2009): 21–38.

Southern Baptist Convention. "Annual Church Profile Statistical Summary, 2019." June 4, 2020. https://www.baptistpress.com/resource-library/news/southern-baptist-convention-continues-statistical-decline-floyd-calls-for-rethinking-acp-process.

Spaite, Daniel, and Debbie Salter Goodwin. *Time Bomb in the Church: Defusing Pastoral Burnout.* Kansas City, MO: Beacon Hill, 1999.

Stark, Rodney, and Roger Finke. *Acts of Faith: Explaining the Human Side of Religion*. Berkeley: University of California Press, 2000.

Stewart, Kristin. "Keeping Your Pastor: An Emerging Challenge." *Journal for the Liberal Arts and Sciences* 13, no. 3 (2009): 112–127.

Studying Congregations website. Accessed July 30, 2021. https://studyingcongregations.org/.

Sullivan, Teresa A., Elizabeth Warren, and Jay Lawrence Westbrook. *The Fragile Middle Class: Americans in Debt*. New Haven, CT: Yale University Press, 2020.

Swidler, Ann. "Culture in Action: Symbols and Strategies." *American Sociological Review* 51, no. 2 (April 1, 1986): 273–286. https://doi.org/10.2307/2095521.

Swoboda, A. J. *The Dusty Ones: Why Wandering Deepens Your Faith*. Grand Rapids, MI: Baker, 2016.

Thiessen, Joel, and Sarah Wilkins-Laflamme. *None of the Above*. New York: NYU Press, 2020.

Tozer, A. W. *The Pursuit of God*. Updated ed. Abbotsford, WI: Aneko, 2015.

Treadgold, Richard. "Transcendent Vocations: Their Relationship to Stress, Depression, and Clarity of Self-Concept." *Journal of Humanistic Psychology* 39, no. 1 (January 1, 1999): 81–105. https://doi.org/10.1177/0022167899391010.

Turton, Douglas W. *Clergy Burnout and Emotional Exhaustion: A Socio-psychological Study of Job Stress and Job Satisfaction*. Lewiston, NY: Edwin Mellen, 2010.

US Bureau of Labor Statistics. "Occupational Employment and Wage Statistics: Clergy." 2021. https://www.bls.gov/oes/current/oes212011.htm.

Voas, David, and Mark Chaves. "Even Intense Religiosity Is Declining in the United States: Comment." *Sociological*

Science 5 (November 15, 2018): 694–710. https://doi.org/ 10.15195/v5.a29.

————. "Is the United States a Counterexample to the Secularization Thesis?" *American Journal of Sociology* 121, no. 5 (March 1, 2016): 1517–1556. https://doi.org/10.1086/ 684202.

Warner, R. Stephen. "The Place of the Congregation in the Contemporary American Religious Configuration." In *American Congregations*. Vol. 2, *New Perspectives in the Study of Congregations*, edited by James P. Wind and James W. Lewis, 54–99. Chicago: University of Chicago Press, 1994.

Weber, Max. *Economy and Society*. Berkeley: University of California Press, 1978.

————. *The Protestant Ethic and the Spirit of Capitalism*. Translated by Stephen Kalberg. Rev. 1920 ed. New York: Oxford University Press, 2011.

Wellman, James K. *Evangelical vs. Liberal: The Clash of Christian Cultures in the Pacific Northwest*. New York: Oxford University Press, 2008.

Wingfield, Mark. "SBC Loses Another 435,000 Members in 2020." Baptist News Global, May 24, 2021. https:// baptistnews.com/article/sbc-loses-another-435000 -members-in-2020/.

Wood, Alex M., P. Alex Linley, John Maltby, Michael Baliousis, and Stephen Joseph. "The Authentic Personality: A Theoretical and Empirical Conceptualization and the Development of the Authenticity Scale." *Journal of Counseling Psychology* 55, no. 3 (2008): 385–399. https://doi .org/10.1037/0022-0167.55.3.385.

Wrzesniewski, Amy, Clark McCauley, Paul Rozin, and Barry Schwartz. "Jobs, Careers, and Callings: People's Relations to Their Work." *Journal of Research in Personality* 31, no. 1

(March 1, 1997): 21–33. https://doi.org/10.1006/jrpe
.1997.2162.

Yang, Fenggang, and Helen Rose Ebaugh. "Transformations
in New Immigrant Religions and Their Global Implications." *American Sociological Review* 66, no. 2 (April 1,
2001): 269–288. https://doi.org/10.2307/2657418.